HAUNTED
GUILDFORD

PHILIP HUTCHINSON

The
History
Press

For Mum and Dad
(because everyone should have a book dedicated to
them at least once in their lives)

Frontispiece: *Guildford High Street, c. 1900.*

First published in 2006 by Tempus Publishing

Reprinted in 2009 by
The History Press
The Mill, Brimscombe Port,
Stroud, Gloucestershire, GL5 2QG
www.thehistorypress.co.uk

British Library Cataloguing in Publication Data.
A catalogue record for this book is available from the British Library.

ISBN 978 0 7524 3826 9

Typesetting and origination by
Tempus Publishing Limited.
Printed in Great Britain.

CONTENTS

Philip Hutchinson. (Simon Drake)

ABOUT THE AUTHOR

Philip Hutchinson was born and brought up in Hampshire but has lived in Guildford for some years. His interest in ghosts goes back to his early childhood but beyond a childhood interest in scary stories he has been unable to explain why.

He trained as an actor at the Academy of Live and Recorded Arts in London and has worked on stages throughout the country. From 2000–02 he was a Council Member of Equity.

In 2000 he was invited to join The Ghost Club, the oldest paranormal society in the world and for several years has sat on the Council of the organisation and taken part in many paranormal investigations at notorious locations. Surprisingly, he is mostly sceptical but has nevertheless seen ghosts on several occasions.

Philip founded The Ghost Tour of Guildford in 2001 and many thousands of people have since followed his eccentric and popular guided walks through Guildford's streets. He has been interviewed for various newspapers, magazines and on radio and television about his work.

He is also a guide at The South Street Caves in Dorking and one of the best known Jack The Ripper tour guides in the world, having delivered papers on the paranormal aspects of the case at major conferences. Philip has acted as the Senior Custodian of Guildford Castle Keep for Guildford Borough Council since 1994 and occasionally works at Guildford Museum.

This is Philip's first exclusive work in print but he has contributed to several books on the paranormal in the past and is the author of several talking books on audio cassette, *Odiham Castle*, *Guildford Castle*, *Wintney Priory* and *The Ghosts of Hart*.

The Ghost Tour of Guildford runs every Friday night from the start of March to the end of October – and Halloween itself – at 8.00 p.m. by the central steps of Holy Trinity church at the top of the pedestrianised High Street. The tours last until 9.45 p.m., finishing at the Angel Hotel and run regardless of the weather. There is no need to book in advance. Private group bookings can be arranged at any time of year. For further details and prices please visit the website at www.ghosttourofguildford.co.uk or phone 01483 506232.

INTRODUCTION AND ACKNOWLEDGEMENTS

England is the most haunted country in the world. Surrey is said to be the most haunted county in England and Guildford is Surrey's historic county town. Authors of paranormal books thirty years ago would have dismissed Guildford as being remarkably bereft of ghosts for a town of its age. This simply isn't true. In researching this book I would often visit a shop or pub to speak to the staff only to be told two new stories about previously unknown sites. Although in recent years the town has received more acknowledgement of its paranormal contributions, this is the first ever book dealing exclusively with 'haunted' Guildford. All illustrations, unless otherwise noted, are copyright of the author.

I would like to give my thanks to the following people: David Rose, Sarah Darnell, Tina Cook, Roger Ness, Julie at the Live & Let Live, Matthew Alexander, Harry at the Tudor Rose, Jane at the Three Pigeons, Vicky at Jigsaw, Debbie and Georgina Cutten, Helen and Bobby Bell, Mark Havler, Helen Fullerton, James Bushell, Janet at the Edinburgh Woollen Mill, Darren Woodyer, Mark Schofield, and the many people who have given me their time and stories with a request they remain anonymous. You know who you are – and so do the ghosts.

Philip Hutchinson
January 2006

Chapter One

THE HIGH STREET

Get that horse out of here!

The Royal Grammar School, High Street

Close to the top of the High Street is the Edward VI Royal Grammar School, founded by a wealthy London merchant called Robert Beckingham in 1509. Edward VI was actually not responsible for the school; he merely re-endowed it in 1551 and the current 'big school' was completed in 1586. It contains one of the more impressive chained libraries in England, the books having been the collection of John Parkhurst. He came from a Guildford family and was a sixteenth-century Bishop of Norwich. A major fire in December 1962 shut the 'big school' for three years but a new school building was erected on the opposite side of the street in 1964, on the site of the former Allen House.

Around 100 years ago, when the school still had boarders, one of the boys was astounded to see one of his father's employees – a groom – walk into a classroom at the school and then suddenly disappear. The following morning a telegram arrived from the boy's father saying that at the same time that previous afternoon, that very groom had been tragically killed in a coaching accident eight miles away from the school. Another version of the same story claims this occurred a long time previous to that. In this account the boy was awake in the dormitory in the garret above the school and he saw a shadow, which he claimed was that of the groom, walking along the wall.

There is also a tale that is spoken about by some of the students today. Accounts vary; some say it refers to an eccentric old master and others maintain it was a rebellious student. The date is also vague but the popular consensus seems to be somewhere in the 1920s. Someone, at some stage, was said to have ridden a horse down one of the staircases in the 'old school'. It is said by some that it was something that would be done on a regular basis, others say it was done once and others embellish this by claiming the horse collapsed and killed the rider during the attempt. Whatever the truth of this story, some of the boys still speak about the ghost who is seen and heard riding a horse down the staircase – I've even heard he is headless! On speaking to the school's archivist, I was told that the story was almost certainly a modern urban myth and he had never heard it. The main staircase in 'big school' is too small and the turn on them too tight to have ridden a horse down. Another version claims that the horseman is not in the school itself at all but rides past it (which does seem more likely, though less interesting). He is said to be a huntsman on a grey steed galloping by the building. It has been suggested that he was one of the 'old boys' of the school, killed while out hunting.

The Royal Grammar School, c. 1900.

Would you like to swing on a light fitting?

The Three Pigeons pub, No. 169 High Street

The Three Pigeons public house is one of the friendliest pubs in the town. It was originally a seventeenth-century blacksmith's and became a pub under the Betts family in 1764 but was partially destroyed in an arson attack on the building next door in 1916. The owners of the adjoining building had recently joined the Temperance Movement and disposed of all their alcohol. It was suggested that the fire was the result of a disgruntled drinker making his opinions clear (obviously showing how clearly he was thinking by setting a fire that damaged the pub next door).

The hauntings there are far more recent, beginning during the long, hot summer of 1976 when a poltergeist (or 'noisy spirit') took up residence in the bar. Every evening between 4.00 and 6.00 p.m. the lights in the bar would turn themselves off and on and the pub cat refused to mount the stairs between the second floor and the garret roof space. It was said that on that staircase at shortly after 1.00 a.m. every night the light fitting would slowly begin to swing from side to side, getting more and more intense, before eventually slowing down and stopping.

The Three Pigeons pub.

The swinging light fitting.

In 2001 I met a man who had worked there himself at that time. He told me that shortly after closing one night he and several other members of staff decided to see if the rumours were true. They sat on the staircase, whiling away the hours and then one of them looked down to his watch and saw the time was shortly after 1.00 in the morning. They looked up to the light fitting and, sure enough, it was slowly swinging from side to side before eventually slowing down and stopping.

The staff say strange things still happen there. Often between 4.00 and 6.00 in the evening the lights in the bar will turn themselves off for a few minutes and then back on, the electrics keep breaking down in the kitchen and there's a strange atmosphere in the room (the kitchen is next to the haunted staircase). In January 2003 Scott MacDonald, the assistant manager, went down to the cellar to turn on some beer barrels but when he returned upstairs to the bar a moment later, someone had turned them all off again.

However, none of this can match what happened in 1988 when the poltergeist was extremely active. Again the lights would go off and on in the bar. Glasses moved from one end of the counter to the other. A barstool was picked up by an unseen hand and flung through the air. On a particularly Python-esque occasion a large glass bowl of cheese on the counter suddenly exploded but we don't know whether or not it was accompanied by a voice screaming, 'I don't like cheese!'

Monmouth's last night

Abbot's Hospital, High Street

One of the most impressive buildings in Guildford is Abbot's Hospital, situated at the top of the High Street, its façade evocative of Hampton Court Palace in miniature form. It was built under George Abbot, a Guildford man who rose to become Archbishop of Canterbury in the early seventeenth century. He was born in a house at the bottom of the High Street, the site of which is now part of the car park adjoining the George Abbot pub. Abbot unfortunately became the only Archbishop of Canterbury to actually kill someone when he misfired his crossbow while out hunting at Bramshill House in Hampshire, killing the gamekeeper whose ghost – it is said – haunts the tree under which he died to this very day. The foundation stone was laid on 7 April 1619. It is not a hospital in the modern sense but in the old fashioned way; a retirement home for elderly Christian folk of Guildford town, a purpose it still serves to this day. So historic is the structure there is still a statute on the books that says if anyone who lives there is accused of witchcraft they are to be expelled from the building.

The most impressive story connected with the hospital dates from the same century in which it was built. In 1685 the English King Charles II had just died, leaving no legitimate heir to the throne and so his brother, James, was invited to become King. This caused a bit of a problem for the English because – although secretly with Catholic sympathies – openly Charles had been a Protestant. James was openly Catholic and people were scared there would be a return to the old ways – the religious persecutions and executions. So they had the bright idea of sending for help from France to James Scott, the Duke of Monmouth (Charles' favourite illegitimate son, a fierce Protestant who was living there).

They asked him to come back to England, march on London, seize the crown as his own and lead his fallen people in their hour of need. He heeded their call and landed at Lyme Regis in

Abbot's Hospital in the 1880s.

Dorset with 150 followers, armed with no more than pitchforks and clubs. Slowly but surely they began to make their way towards London, but no sooner had they begun than word reached James II of their intentions. He sent the English army to capture them and at the Battle of Sedgemoor in 1685 Monmouth's troops were entirely routed. The infamous 'hanging judge', Judge Jeffreys, said he would turn Somerset into a sea of blood and he very nearly succeeded as so many of Monmouth's followers were hanged, drawn and quartered. This fate didn't await the Duke of Monmouth, as he managed to escape at the Battle of Sedgemoor but was found a few days later hiding in a bush, given away – it is said – by his twinkling eyes.

Day by day, night by night and stage by stage he was taken back to London – to the Tower – to await his trial for treason and subsequent execution. Being a member of the aristocracy he wasn't strung up like the *hoi polloi* would have been. Being of noble birth he was 'allowed' to just have his head cut off. Unfortunately for him, his executioner was the infamous Jack Ketch; 6' 7" tall, 18 stones in weight and a man with more bungles to his name than a whole series of *Rainbow*.

Come the day of Monmouth's execution, he tipped Ketch as was the custom and said, 'Prithee, let me feel the axe. I fear it is not sharp enough'. He lay his head upon the block, Jack Ketch swung the axe up in the air, threw it down ... and cut into the back of Monmouth's shoulders. It is said Monmouth turned his head and stared at Ketch with reproachful eyes. Ketch withdrew the axe and swung down again, splitting into the back of Monmouth's skull. He hit down a third time, a fourth time and a fifth time and still the Duke of Monmouth's head was not entirely severed from his shoulders. Jack Ketch threw down the axe and yelled, 'God damn me, I can do no more. I have not the heart' but he was forced to continue. With nothing left to do, his axe now firmly blunted, Jack Ketch reached into his pocket, pulled out his pocket knife and began to cut away what was left of the Duke of Monmouth's head.

Immediately after his execution it was realised that no portrait of the man had been made while he was alive and being a member of the Royal Family this had to be rectified. So his bloody head was quickly recovered, given a quick wash with a rag, crudely sewn onto his stump of a neck and a large ruff placed around it to hide the ugly scar. His portrait was painted posthumously and remains in the National Portrait Gallery in London looking a little green around the gills.

That night the Duke of Monmouth's headless ghost was seen at the Playhouse in London – his favourite haunt while alive – and at every spot in which he had been confined during his journey back to the Tower and his death. The room at the top front of the gatehouse used to be called The Muniment Room. It is now named the Monmouth Room, as it is the very last place the Duke of Monmouth spent a night, on 12 July 1685, before reaching the Tower and his early demise and, we suppose, where he returned momentarily – without his head – after his death.

The building also presents us with a minor second story. In the early years of the 1900s an elderly man who lived in a room at the rear of the courtyard found himself frequently woken at night by the sound of trumpet music and raucous partying coming from further down the corridor. Without fail, every time he got out of bed to investigate, he would be greeted by silence as soon as he opened the door. Nothing else has been reported there for many years.

Ladies who lunch

The Tudor Rose restaurant, No. 144 High Street

Overlooking the High Street is one of Guildford's most well-loved establishments, the Tudor Rose. It can only be reached via the very narrow and mysterious old boarded alleyway (Milkhouse Gate) and then up another narrow and steep staircase into the restaurant itself but it is a journey worth making. The owner, Harry and his staff have a very positive reputation that is well earned.

There is no doubt the building is very old; inside the restaurant there are low ceilings and many exposed old beams. In the 1990s an engineer was working in the cellar of the building, which doesn't belong to the restaurant. He had arrived very early in the morning and had just put down his bag of tools on the floor when he saw the bottom half of a grey dress and a pair of shoed feet nimbly padding up the stairs. It was only there for a second and then gone.

During my visit to the restaurant, Harry told me that the dishwasher, which has to be operated by pushing a button and holding it in for several seconds, can sometimes operate of its own accord. He also mentioned two ghost sightings. The first had happened a few years ago before he took over. A company rep had come in for a meeting with the previous owner and while sitting in the main restaurant on the first floor, he had suddenly turned as white as a sheet. When asked if he was feeling unwell, he said he had noticed a little woman sitting in the wooden seat between the two front windows and she had just disappeared before his eyes.

In early 2005 some external work was done on the building and scaffolding was put up around the front. Either as a record of his handiwork, or to show friends what he was doing, one of the young builders stood at the far end of the scaffolding and took a photo of the window on the right. There was no one in the restaurant at the time he took the picture. However, later on, after uploading the image onto his computer and looking at it more closely he saw a woman at the window looking out at him.

Above: *The Tudor Rose restaurant.*

Left: *The haunted seat.*

Keeping an eye on the new boy

Jeffrey & Sons, formerly at Nos 132-134 High Street

At the time of publication, the building two doors up from Tunsgate Arch is a branch of the ladies' clothing store, Jigsaw. The narrow frontage gives no indication of the huge expanse of this nicely presented shop once you get inside. Up to 2001 (when, with much publicity and sadness, its doors closed for the last time) it was Jeffrey & Sons sports shop. The Jeffrey family originally came to Guildford from Plymouth in 1851, setting up a gun shop opposite Holy Trinity church. In 1863 the shop moved to No. 132 High Street, which had formerly been the eighteenth-century Green Man Inn. The bricked-up cellars from that time still exist under the street paving. Being a family business, the Jeffreys lived in luxurious accommodation directly above the shop. The building also had one of the very few gardens in the High Street and its own swimming pool. The door to the right leads up to the living area. In 1928 Harold Jeffrey took over ownership of the shop and his brother Jack acted as a Company Director. Harold was a very well-known local character. He was one of the first Scouts in the country and met Lord Baden-Powell on many occasions. He is buried at the Mount Cemetery, having died in 1970. Jack died in 1977 and the story dates from two years later, in 1979.

A young man by the name of Nick Hill had just started at Jeffrey's and was on his first day of work. During the morning the Manager, Mr Hall, had shown him around the building; where the stock was kept, how to work the cash till and how to speak to the customers without using strings of four-letter words. Come that afternoon, he was confident enough to send Nick Hill to the stock room in the basement to get some things. To get there, Nick Hill had to pass the company office and on doing so he saw the door was ajar. Sitting inside he saw an old man he'd not been introduced to that morning, sat at a desk with a brown and white checked jacket, brushed-back white hair and reading a broadsheet newspaper.

Nick Hill studied him for a moment and decided the polite thing to do would be to say 'Hello' but as soon as he stuck his head round the threshold of the door, the old man dissolved before his eyes and the air became cold and musty. Nick Hill ran back to Mr Hall. He told him what he'd just seen. He spoke of the old man in the office, the brown and white checked jacket, the brushed-back white hair and the broadsheet newspaper. He described his face in detail. And now it was Mr Hall's turn to be surprised. He said, 'That's Jack Jeffrey. He died two years ago'. The office had been used by Jack Jeffrey as his own personal 'den' after his retirement and he used to sit in there each day reading the papers. Perhaps he was coming back to check on the new employee?

When the building was used by Jeffrey's the top floor was always locked. Previously it had been used to store the guns and on occasion, staff had seen the firearms moving around the room of their own volition.

In January 2006 I visited the shop to speak to the staff about their ghost. They were extremely friendly and helpful but knew nothing about it. I was amazed when I found out that none of them had even been down in the cellar. I was allowed to go down there myself to take a photograph. The manageress directed me to a doormat at a fenced-off area near the front of the shop and removed a large board over a hole in the floor. A small ladder led down into the dark and dusty cellar and I was very saddened by what I found.

The cellar is only about 5ft high today. The whitewashed bricks are similar to many other cellars I have seen around the High Street and are hundreds of years old. There is nothing down

The old Jeffrey's shop before the refit.

The cellar of Jeffrey's.

there now and no sign of any old walls where Jack Jeffrey's 'den' might once have been. Just one small, empty space that stretches about halfway under the current shop. It is not at all what I had imagined.

A miscarriage of justice?

Tunsgate Arch, High Street

This most tragic of stories begins in 1684 with the birth, in Wisborough Green, Sussex, of a boy by the name of Christopher Slaughterford. At the age of fourteen he was apprenticed to a Mr Dayer of Godalming, a maltster. He was there for three years and then returned to his parents. He worked for several other employers on the Surrey and Sussex borders and on coming of age he took the malt house at Shalford with his aunt as a housekeeper, an apprentice and a lodger to help pay the way. By now being a young man with some money he turned his attentions towards a local servant girl – a girl from Compton by the name of Jane Young. Although Jane and her family were poor she was considered quite a catch. She was a good-looking girl and kind natured. She had been employed by a woman called Elizabeth Chapman and had recently told her she was about to leave her service as she was to marry Slaughterford.

The Three Tuns shortly before demolition (from In And Around Guildford, *1895).*

On 5 October 1708 the pair were seen walking together in the grounds of Loseley Park near Guildford but that evening Slaughterford returned home alone. There was no sign of Jane. People began to ask questions of him. 'Where was she?' or – more jokingly – 'Have you killed her?' Day by day went by and there was still no sign of the missing girl. Now people were getting very suspicious of Slaughterford and so he voluntarily went before two Justices of the Peace – a Captain Boothby and a Mr Fulham. When they finished listening to him they told him to go home and wait for Jane. He'd done nothing wrong and she'd turn up in due course. And turn up she did.

In early November the decomposing, strangled, battered body of Jane Young was found lying face down in a sandpit in Loseley Park. Now the Slaughterford accusations began in earnest. Everyone was convinced he'd killed her, so he went before another Justice of the Peace and demanded that he stand trial to clear his name once and for all. Reluctantly it was agreed. He was sent to the Marshalsea Prison in London, his trial was held at the Kingston Assizes under Justice Worth and at the end of the trial he was acquitted. Set free, an innocent man, he was told to go away and rebuild his life.

At this stage Christopher Slaughterford could have left Guildford. He could have gone elsewhere in the country where no one knew his name. But he didn't. So adamant was he that he'd done nothing wrong that he stayed there and this was his fatal error. By this time the friends and family of Jane Young – although they were poor – were able to raise enough money to hold a second trial; a private prosecution on appeal. Jane's brother, Henry Young, formally lodged an appeal in an attempt to convict a man whose case had already been dismissed by magistrates and found not guilty at trial.

Slaughterford was taken back into custody. This trial was held at the Queen's Bench Bar in Westminster under Lord Chief Justice Holt and at this trial, although the witnesses and evidence

Slaughterford's execution from The Guildford Jackdaw.

were the same as the first trial, he was found guilty of Jane Young's murder and sentenced to be hanged by the neck until he was dead.

Now there's a strange irony to this. Had he been found guilty at his first trial his life would almost certainly have been spared because all the evidence against him was purely circumstantial. However, there was a strange law in the time of Queen Anne which said if anyone was found guilty of a crime at a private prosecution then – because it was not a State Case – the monarch had no right to intercede. This means in short because he was found innocent at his first trial but guilty at the second he was now going to die and there was nothing anyone could do to stop it.

Three ministers were sent to him to urge him to confess but each time one was sent it only strengthened his resolve he'd done nothing wrong. On Friday 30 June, Slaughterford was brought back to Guildford to wait in Guildford's House of Correction. Some accounts say he was kept in the Three Tuns or the White Lyon in Guildford High Street but this makes no sense – why keep a convicted murderer in a pub when there is a secure prison almost next door? The White Lyon references are probably confusing it with the tavern next door to the Marshalsea Prison where he'd been held. He even earned a few days reprieve for him to confess to a Mr Woodroff, a Guildford preacher but all he did was inform the man he was innocent. Early in the morning on Sunday 9 July 1709 he was brought on the back of a cart up Guildford High Street to where a gallows had been erected in the yard of the Three Tuns Inn (now occupied by Tunsgate Arch) – the final execution ever to be held in Guildford High Street.

Slaughterford dismounted the cart and gave a signed deposition to the Sheriff of Guildford protesting his innocence. Part of it read:

Being brought here to die ... I thought myself obliged to let the world know ... that I know nothing of the death of Jane Young, nor how she came by her death – directly or indirectly... However, I freely forgive all my enemies and pray to God to give them a due sense of their errors and in due time to bring the truth to light.

Upon presentation, Slaughterford mounted the scaffold, constructed by Edward Tinmore for £2 16s but before the executioner had a chance to turn him off the ladder Slaughterford jumped off first, effectively committing suicide before he could be executed and launching himself into eternity. It's unsettling to realise the spectators would then have made their way to church for Sunday Service.

Two nights later, on 11 July, Slaughterford came back. One of the chief accusers at his trial – a man by the name of Roger Valler – was walking home along Tunsgate, yards from the execution spot, when he suddenly felt a cold breeze down the back of his neck. He turned around and was confronted in the moonlight by the ghost of Christopher Slaughterford, a flaming torch in one hand and a club in the other with a cut noose round his neck blowing in a breeze that wasn't there. The ghost was wearing the clothes Slaughterford had worn in life and was said to be crying, 'Vengeance! Vengeance!' Roger Valler began to run home, followed closely behind by the ghost which, although not moving, was always only a couple of feet behind him and only disappeared in a flash of fire when Valler had got in through his front door, bolting it, driven (it is said) half to madness. Accounts say he stayed in bed for days afterwards, too scared to leave the house. Valler must have been a man of substance because clearly marked on the Guildford ichnography of 1739, opposite the current Sydenham Road car park, is a large patch of ground marked 'Roger Valler's field'.

At the same time Slaughterford's ghost appeared to his servant, Joseph Lee, who was at the bottom of the High Street, this time carrying a sword instead of a club, saying, 'Oh, cruel Joseph!' three times before walking down The Shambles. At the same time his ghost was also seen by his aunt, who had been milking a cow at the malt house in Shalford and who tried to talk to him. The ghost appeared to be as solid and real as a living person. All he could do was shake his head and point to the rope around his neck, his eyes full of tears. Also on that Tuesday night his ghost was seen yet again. He appeared at the Marshalsea Prison in London where he'd been confined and heard rattling his fetters by drinkers at the White Lyon Tavern next door (or in Guildford High Street). Other accounts mention him being seen at the sandpit in Loseley Park where Jane Young's body had been found and in the courtyard of the Three Tuns Inn, where two days before the Approved Men of Guildford had stood and watched him die. So many appearances in different places – I think it's fairly safe to say he didn't travel by train. Tales of Slaughterford's ghost – and perceived guilt – were still apparent by the end of the eighteenth century as recounted in the small cautionary tale *The Guildford Jackdaw* from 1794:

I ... had heard of a strange story of [a] man's ghost, walking in a pit, before you come to Loseley ... a murder had been committed in this place so many years since and the man was hanged at the market-house in the town of Guildford.

This wasn't the last time he was seen in Guildford, for on 12 June 1994 the local film group Circle Eight were making their latest feature called *Tales Of The Pilgrims' Way*. As part of this film they told Slaughterford's story; his courting of Jane Young, her murder, his trial, execution and haunting of Tunsgate Arch. That morning the High Street was closed to pedestrians and traffic. Straw was lain over the setts, people in period costume milled about, a large gallows was erected

Slaughterford's ghost from a contemporary chap-book.

in front of the Guildhall and Slaughterford died again – but this time for the cameras. The actual hanging sequence had to be shot in a great hurry as the crew only had police clearance until 9.00 a.m. so it had be achieved in one shot. By complete coincidence, the moment the actor's body fell and he was 'hanged' the bells of the Guildhall chimed the hour – the exact time of day at which people were hanged in England. It was also a Sunday. The chilling irony of the moment was not lost on the actor playing Slaughterford as he dangled from a concealed harness. It was me.

Many people have now reached the conclusion that Slaughterford died an innocent man. I am less sure. No one else was ever suspected of the crime and he was seen with Jane Young on the night she died. It is indeed unlikely that Christopher Slaughterford murdered her but that is all the information we have to make judgement. Had his trial been held in the twenty-first century, however, with this information it would have been dismissed immediately.

Too many rooms to swing a cat

Kew, No. 122 High Street

This tale is one of the most mysterious in Guildford. It has been infuriating to research, as it is unlikely we will ever know the real location of the haunting with 100 per cent certainty. The problem is that it could refer to any one of four buildings in two different spots on the High Street. The High Street was renumbered on 1 January 1961 and although the previous and

Number 122 High Street.

current numbers are easy to place, records don't show if these numbers refer to the earlier or later system. Also, some details can only belong to one building, where other details are known to belong to another. Maybe there were similar hauntings in several buildings?

I have personally concluded that the building in question is actually the present-day No. 122, the middle part of the ancient whitewashed building just below Tunsgate Arch. They may well be the oldest domestic buildings in Guildford, parts of the interior dating maybe from the thirteenth century but the façade from the sixteenth century – old photographs show it resplendent with the date 1536. On New Year's Day in 1922 the building was severely damaged by fire but the family living above the shop managed to escape unharmed. During the reconstruction the builders removed an alleyway called Lyon's Gate, like many others in Guildford, running between the gable closest to Tunsgate Arch and the two lower ones. The first time I was told the tale I was informed this was the building in question and some of the later events completely rule out the other candidates. However, I will give them due credit – just in case.

In 1953 the shop underneath the central gable was being turned into a ladies' clothing shop. Some accounts put the date as 1963 and the building as previously being a butcher's – if that is the case, then the building would have to be the modern No. 92 which is a white building

Numbers 92 and 90 High Street.

further down the street with a bay window on the first floor. Kelly's Directory shows it as being Read & Co. the butchers earlier in the century. Curiously, on No. 92 there is no second floor. There appears to be but it is entirely cosmetic. When the building was constructed the lack of a second floor broke up the line of the High Street and so a blank wall was raised above it and a fake window inserted where a second floor would be. To confuse matters further, this building was indeed No. 122 High Street until 1961 and on postcards from the turn of the century the building between the current day No. 122 and Tunsgate Arch was also a butcher's shop. The muddle will get worse as the story progresses!

The builders came to Guildford each morning from London. A few of them decided to save their train fares and get the job completed more quickly by staying on site overnight rather than commuting back and forth every day. For a couple of nights they had slept in sleeping bags on the ground floor but then, on the third night, something unusual happened. In the early hours of the morning the workmen were awakened by a sound coming from above their heads. It was the sound of a woman talking and then sobbing, coming from a room which had been bricked up a long time before – maybe at the time the building was repaired following the 1922 fire. Then the sobbing stopped and was replaced with the sound of footsteps. Slow, heavy, limping footsteps walking round and round the bricked-up room above them. Then the footsteps passed straight through the solid wall and out onto the landing. A door was heard swinging upstairs, yet all the doors had been removed. By this time the footsteps were so close the workmen could also hear the rustle of crinoline skirts. The footsteps got closer and closer and then suddenly stopped at the top of the stairs. The workmen hardly dared to breathe, wondering what was going to happen next. Then the footsteps began again; slow, heavy, limping footsteps walking down the stairs into the room in which the petrified men stood. Down a staircase they'd taken out the day before!

They were more than a little scared and so the following morning the foreman ordered the bricked-up room to be opened. When the workmen got inside they found a Tudor fireplace and window. It was said there was another bricked up part of the building and when the workmen got in there they found another Tudor window and the skeletal remains of no less than eight cats. Unusual, you may think but not really. At this time it was popular when constructing a new building to put a cat in the wall cavity to ward off evil spirits. Dead or alive wasn't important – if they weren't dead to start with, they soon would be. Many old buildings being converted to this day are sometimes found with a skeletal or mummified cat inside. To find one is quite usual but eight? They must have thought there was something very nasty to keep at bay there.

This is where things get even more confusing. The Corona Café used to be at No. 121 High Street (the present No. 90 High Street). The Corona, a well-loved business, closed in 1978 and was replaced by a branch of Pizzaland. In 1984 the old building was undergoing repair works and hidden in the walls and under the floors workmen found shoes, clay pipes, dried gorse, an eighteenth-century account book, the skeletons of many rats – and a cat. A coin had previously been found on top of one of the beams, dating from 1490. This much we know is undeniable. The Corona Café stood next to the building with the bay window and the false second floor, which was No. 122 High Street in 1953. A gentleman told one of my colleagues that he had been walking up the stairs in the old Corona building when he felt a strange atmosphere. On asking if the building was haunted he was told that members of staff had seen a shady shape on the top floor and heard footsteps on the stairs. Are the stories from several buildings being fused into one? I've been given an account by a local woman who claims that the current Sainsbury's was a butcher's shop fifty years ago and on knocking down a wall the workmen found the skeletons of half a man and half a horse which received a lot of press coverage. Sainsbury's has been in the same position for 100 years now and prior to that it was the White Hart Inn, so she has the wrong location and is almost certainly thinking of the No. 122 High Street renovations. As for finding the skeletons of half a man and half a horse, well now we know what happened to Mr Tumnus after he left Narnia. Sadly, no interesting wardrobes were found nearby…

A local historian also told me that the Ealing Psychical Research Society were called in to conduct an investigation at the site. The founder of this group was a friend of mine – the late author Andrew Green. Andrew told me he had never even heard of the building, or any of the others it may have been, though he lived just outside Guildford for many years.

In 1985 the hauntings began again. Three girls from the Guildford School of Acting were renting the first-floor apartment. Two of the girls shared a large bedroom, the third having a smaller box room to herself. Late one night she was awakened by, walking round her bed, the sound of slow, heavy, limping footsteps and the rustling of crinoline skirts. She screamed, her two friends came running in to ask what was wrong but before they had a chance they too heard the footsteps – and that night they all slept together cosily in the other bedroom. Then a dim blue light began to appear at the top of the staircase which grew stronger and stronger with each successive night until it was eventually as strong as a torch beam. The girls, able to bear no more, called in a priest to hold a blessing at the site and the hauntings stopped – or did they?

In the summer of 2005 I was told by one of the current residents of that apartment that she had entered the living room in the morning a few days previously and an unknown black cat had zoomed past her and out of the door.

So, to nail down the story, there is a very good reason why I believe the haunting had to be at the modern No. 122 High Street. The tale mentions students living above the shop in 1985 being scared by the same phenomena as had occurred thirty-two years previously. It cannot be where the Corona Café used to be, because the first floor was always part of the public area. It cannot be the building with the bay window as that floor has always been used as the stock room or offices for the shop underneath (and incidentally, there have been rumours of people seeing things or having their clothes tugged in this room). That only leaves the modern No. 122 by Tunsgate Arch. The first floor has been used as student accommodation for many years and the tenants seem to change every year.

Fright club

Russell & Bromley, Nos 84-86 High Street

Russell & Bromley are listed as being on this site by the 1930s but some people well remember the time in the 1950s and '60s when the first floor of the building was used as a club run by a man called John Dromfield. It was called the Tunsgate Club but was also commonly referred to as the Dromfield Club. It was mainly a drinking club but it did also once have a dancefloor. Even today it is clear to see that the front of the building is wider than that of many others in the High Street, showing that it once had grander aspirations. The shoe chain has been there for over seventy years now but in the 1930s a solicitors' firm was on the first floor. This became the Galleon Club in the 1940s and was The Tunsgate Club by 1957. It shut in 1970 and by 1973 Russell & Bromley had taken over the entire building.

For some decades the staff were aware of a story that during the building's days as a centre of entertainment, somebody – but they didn't know who – had hanged themselves in one of the rooms at the top of the building. There are also rumours that their cellar, which is locked up today, is haunted by an unquantifiable 'something' and one morning when opening the shop the staff had found that overnight the window display had been drastically altered.

An employee recently told me that at Christmas 2004 she had been walking down the staircase from the stock room. She had been alone up there but when she was a few steps down, a two-pence piece shot out of the room past her and down the stairs. In October 2005 the same employee had been sitting in the staff room reading a magazine in the company of a colleague. From behind her colleague the lid of a drinks bottle suddenly flew off the table and landed between them.

This was during the middle of a period of building work and the builders told me themselves that some strange things had been happening while they were there but they didn't go into detail. It's very interesting to note that many of the most active hauntings in Guildford tend to occur during periods of renovation. It all depends on your interpretation of what ghosts are but it does seem plausible that the workmen are stirring up whatever lies within, either by movement of the fabric of the building, or – if that is your belief – by annoying the ghosts residing there.

The Russell & Bromley shoe shop.

Sleepless nights with soldiers and nuns

The Angel Hotel, No. 91 High Street

There can be no doubt whatsoever that the Angel Hotel is the most famous haunted building in Guildford. Generally speaking if you were to pick up a book on ghosts and see Guildford in the index as you turn to the relevant page you will find an account of this old coaching inn.

The site is definitely ancient but it is almost impossible to deduce its original purpose. What is known is that underneath the building is a thirteenth-century undercroft (very similar to the medieval undercroft in the care of Guildford Borough Council and open to the public in the summer on the other side of the street). It is not known what purpose this one served but they usually acted as shops and the owners lived in the houses above. It has also been suggested that this undercroft (often incorrectly referred to as a crypt) may well have once been part of a

The Angel in the 1930s.

The Angel Yard in 1884.

monastic settlement but such a view has to remain conjectural. Unconfirmed reports of religious wall-paintings being found in the room in the early nineteenth century are what began the stories but it is possible the site was being confused with the paintings that were definitely discovered in St Mary's church at the same time.

Likewise, the name Angel itself is difficult to pinpoint. The Angel was certainly a popular name for Medieval inns but the Fish Cross stood outside here between 1345 and 1595 and it has been suggested this marketplace was once crowned with a stone flying angel. The first written record of the building is from June 1527, when the Fish Cross still stood. It was already by that time a considerable structure containing over a dozen rooms and stabling for nine horses. It also fronted an orchard at this time. It was an inn owned by John Astrete by 1606. It is highly likely that a good deal of the inside of the Angel today is the same building with the same panelling, which makes it a remarkable survival.

By the early 1800s the Angel was a highly respectable establishment and in the 1830s the three-gabled timber façade was refronted with the one we see today. Around this time a Masonic

*A cleaned-up copy of the sketch made
by Mr Dell.*

Lodge was created which met here. Before the coming of the railways to Guildford in 1845 Guildford had several coaching inns because it was halfway on the main road from London to The South Coast, which made it a very convenient overnight stopping point for sailors on shore leave. At one time there could be up to 200 transients in Guildford every night so space was at a premium. However, once the railways put paid to the need for coaches this industry died out and the Angel is the sole survivor of this profitable time. By 1847 the list of rooms was extensive.

Embracing change, in 1906 not only did the Angel have a telephone number (0187) but it was also the HQ of the Automobile Club of Great Britain and Ireland. Work in 1953 revealed a Jacobean fireplace in the main hall, which is still in use. In 1970 the decaying and damp old chalk in the undercroft was replaced with reconstituted stone and it was turned into a restaurant.

In November 1969 a lady guest was staying in The Prince Imperial of France Room (Room 1, now renamed the Freiburg Suite in honour of Guildford's German twin town) which stands at the top front of the building above the archway, the most expensive room in this very exclusive hotel. It was given that name after a visit by the Heir Apparent in 1876, who had stayed in the room. The lady guest phoned down to reception at 8.00 p.m. and the receptionist asked if she could help but the woman didn't reply. Concerned for her welfare, the receptionist put the phone down and went up to Room 1. She knocked on the door and asked the guest if there was any problem but there was still no reply. Now very worried, the receptionist pushed open the door and found the guest standing in the middle of the room, the phone in one hand and the receiver in the other, paralysed with fear. When she had been calmed down, the woman said that there was something in the room. She hadn't seen it or heard it but there was definitely something behind the mirror. She demanded to be moved, which she duly was.

On 31 January 1970, a Mr G. Dell from Bayswater in London was sitting in the restaurant with his wife and beckoned over the manager, Mr Kiersz. He told him what had happened in the early hours of that morning. The previous day, Mr and Mrs Dell had arrived in Guildford for a long weekend break. Some friends had come to visit them at the hotel and they had somewhat overdone the evening meal. When it was time to retire, Mr Dell found he couldn't sleep. He lay tossing and turning in bed for some time, in the way that many people do on their first night in unfamiliar surroundings and eventually resigned himself at 3.00 a.m. to spending the rest of the night sitting in an armchair overlooking the High Street. He would occasionally glance across to his wife who was sound asleep and to do this, his eyeline had to pass a large old wardrobe against the wall adjacent to the window. It had a vast mirror upon it measuring 7 by 4ft and on one of these occasions Mr Dell was astonished to see, staring back at him from behind the mirror and visible only from the waist up, a soldier. He was wearing a mid-nineteenth century Eastern European military uniform and had a large walrus moustache, thinning hair that was brushed back and he was said to be wearing a curious expression.

Mr Dell studied the apparition for a few moments and then when he was quite sure his eyes were not deceiving him he tiptoed over to his wife and woke her. For the next few minutes she could see nothing, then slowly but surely she too saw the figure of the motionless soldier staring back at them from behind the mirror. Over the following twenty minutes Mr Dell had the presence of mind to grab a pen and a red napkin from that evening's meal that lay at his bedside and sketch the figure, willingly posing for them. When a full half-hour had elapsed the figure slowly faded away before their eyes and all was calm again. The manager was astounded. He'd never heard anything of the sort but he did recount what had happened to the lady guest the previous November. The assistant manager, Colin Anderson, also claimed to have seen the soldier himself.

In 1973 the actor Roger Moore was staying at the Angel. He too was staying in Room 1 but his apparition was altogether more unsettling. The first two nights he slept in the room he woke at 2.00 a.m. to find an icy chill and a white, misty figure with arms, legs and head but no features float straight through the solid oak door and up to his bedside. Recovering himself, Roger Moore sat up in bed and quietly asked the ghost if he could help it. As he moved to get out of bed, the figure quickly disappeared. The following night it happened at exactly the same time but now Moore felt more concerned, feeling that perhaps the ghost was after him for some reason. On the third night when he went to bed he found the room's Bible open at the 23rd Psalm (The Lord Is My Shepherd) and that night nothing unusual happened. When he awoke the following morning the maid asked him if he'd been disturbed the previous night. Roger Moore was astounded, because he hadn't spoken of what he'd seen but he calmly replied that he hadn't. It was at this point the maid gestured towards the Bible and said she didn't think he would have been, as the ghost really hated the 23rd Psalm. Apparently, the maid and other members of staff had frequently seen the soldier themselves but how they knew he disliked this particular piece is unknown.

The Angel undercroft, c. 1905.

In 1979 the actress and singer Petula Clark was appearing at the Yvonne Arnaud Theatre and she was staying in Room 1. She too saw the resident soldier staring back at her from behind the mirror during the course of her stay.

In 1985 at the end of October, a waitress called Mary Dibley was disturbed by phantom voices. At 9.30 one evening she had been walking along a corridor when a voice called out to her but no one was there. She passed the laundry room and a bedroom when the same voice called her name again. Mary was rather unnerved after she checked the rooms nearby and discovered them all to be deserted.

At this time, the building was due to be sold off by the Trusthouse Forte Group who made a start by removing all the old furniture. They scrapped the plan but not until a certain piece had coincidentally been disposed of: the large wardrobe from Room 1 was carted away on the back of a skip and the soldier was – apparently – not seen again. One local historian has suggested to me that he feels the soldier may simply have been an old print used on the back of the mirror and if the moonlight shone upon it the right way it could make the picture appear through the reflective backing. I am no physicist, so I can't say if this is possible or not. These apparitions, however, are far from the only ghosts in the Angel.

During alterations in Room 3 next door (variously dated to being anytime in the 1950s or '60s) a priest hole was discovered, or at least a small chamber some have interpreted as being such. A Mr Madden of the Surrey Trust found a bullet lodged in a nearby beam. Legends then began of a fatal duel fought here in the time of the Franco-Prussian war and that the soldier and bullet are remnants of that inexplicable event. Likewise, this may have no sinister connotations and could just be the result of a drunken guest with a pistol firing a bullet into the building. Another tale connected to Room 3 is probably an urban myth and may well be a twist on the story of the Prince Imperial staying in the building. A soldier is supposed to have visited a prince staying at the hotel to plead for the life of his son, who had been condemned to death but the prince refused to help and the son was executed. Since that time, strange events were recorded in the room. Some guests have mentioned that suddenly all outside sounds have disappeared and the walls have seemed to start closing in around them. A few vague stories of an unseen ghost have also been circulated about the room.

And the supernatural roll call continues. In 1998 the TV programme *The Why Files* visited the Angel. The general manager, Grant Barrow, told the crew that six months previously the night manager had called him to the bottom of the staircase saying he could 'smell the nun'. They looked up to the first floor and saw the white outline of a nun moving from left to right. She was accompanied by a very strong smell of lavender and Mr Barrow followed her along the corridor. The floorboards were actually creaking as she walked towards the Brontë Suite and then disappeared. An hour later they smelt the lavender again. The TV crew called in a medium, who felt a strong energy along the first floor gallery suggesting the actual wood of the structure retained something. On entering the Freiburg Suite she felt the energy was at its peak. One has to question if she really did feel these things or had just done some reading on the building beforehand. As Matthew Alexander of Guildford Museum rightly pointed out at the time, there is no evidence of there really being a monastic establishment here and any woman from the Medieval period who looked like a nun may not be a nun at all. It was the standard mode of dress for a married woman. Also, why would a Medieval nun be walking up and down a staircase which, at the earliest, is Jacobean – especially as she is then heard creaking on the floorboards of a post-Medieval building? The staff have seen her on several occasions, either at the top of the main stairs or floating down the staircase into the restaurant in the undercroft, which frequently experiences sharp drops in temperature. The standard and completely fake story applies to the Angel as it does to dozens of other sites in Britain. Apparently this had indeed once been a monastery and a nun fell in love with a monk, for which crime she was bricked up alive (murder, of course, being a mortal sin). She now floats throughout the building in a lost bid to escape her confinement. Cooking utensils and other items have supposedly been seen moving by themselves in the undercroft and sometimes the sound of footsteps. An unknown male figure has also been seen floating through the restaurant.

Tales further circulate of an old man periodically seen calmly sitting by the fireplace in the main lounge. In 2003 a paranormal group picked up voices on recording equipment left in the William Moore Room. As late as September 2002 a man had been seen walking into one of the bedrooms, looking out of the window and then turning and walking through the door again. Andrew Green collected several accounts with the names of the witnesses over the years of this particular ghost. Another witness saw one of the chairs in a bedroom suddenly shift itself six inches towards the window.

In regards to the nun, a current employee who had seen and smelt the ghost himself told a story to a colleague of mine – she wasn't a nun at all: as far as he had seen, her clothing was from the 1600s. This would fit in with what we know about the building. He also claims to have seen the soldier, thought to have left the building in the 1980s and both he and his sister had seen a spectral butler in one of the front bedrooms. Another chambermaid in the 1980s was cleaning Room 1 when a small tabby cat appeared from nowhere and darted past her out of the door.

In 1989 the unthinkable happened when The Angel was shut down with the threat of demolition hanging over it. After re-opening it is now one of the town's biggest comeback candidates.

Where's George?

Robert Dyas, formerly at Nos 71-73 High Street

Robert Dyas moved into White Lion Walk a few years ago. Before that they had a store on the spot of the High Street where Ottakar's bookshop stands in 2006. Robert Dyas were supposed to have had a poltergeist in the cellar of the building which played havoc with the electrics and threw stock around, both when it was empty and at members of staff.

I spoke to a man who had been employed by the company for forty years and had started working at the High Street branch in the early 1960s. Even then, the staff used to joke about their ghost. They called him George and he had been seen on occasion in the cellar walking south, towards the centre of the street where the cellar once joined to that in the opposite building. However, by the 1960s a large part had been bricked up and George was supposed to walk through the wall to the other side (in more ways than one). In spite of all his years there, the employee had never seen anything unusual. George, by the way, is a very common pet name for ghosts whose identity is actually unknown.

Robert Dyas days after the fire in 2001.

Number 59 High Street.

In the summer of 2001 the building was completely gutted by fire. There was a genuine concern it was going to spread to other buildings in the High Street but although the firemen quickly managed to extinguish the flames, the building was virtually destroyed. The smell of burning hung around in the air for days afterwards and when reconstruction began the building was entirely rebuilt leaving only the front. That too was eventually removed and the current shop on the site is entirely new.

Baggage handlers

Salisbury's, formerly at No. 59 High Street

Built onto the east side of White Lion Walk today is a shop currently used by Clinton Cards. White Lion Walk is so named because it is a shopping arcade built on the site of the former White Lion Hotel, an establishment rather similar in size and reputation to the Angel Hotel further up the street. It was demolished in 1957 and was rebuilt as a branch of Woolworths before that in turn gave way to the modern complex in 1986. Replicas of the statue of the original White Lion – only destroyed in recent memory – can still be seen above the entrances onto the High Street and North Street.

In 1996, when the shop was still in use by Salisbury's, the luggage chain, a young man named James Bushell was working there on a six-month contract. It was a Saturday and he was taking his tea break on the first floor with a girl called Alison who worked there at weekends. Suitcases and various items of hand luggage were on display on the walls around them. As they were chatting, they were distracted by a rattling noise coming from one of the displays. To their astonishment a large Samsonite suitcase (not the lightest of items) which had actually been fixed to the wall ripped itself from its moorings and flung itself across the room in their direction.

They were both so shocked by this occurrence that neither could move. Alison gripped the sides of the chair and James found himself momentarily paralysed. Both of them eventually recovered their senses and hurried downstairs. James was informed that things of that nature had been happening in the building for some time and on one occasion a priest was brought in to bless the shop but it had made no difference. One manageress resigned from her position, having complained about the unsettling events and saying the building held something 'very very violent'.

In late 2005, by which time the shop had long been a branch of Clinton Cards, one of the employees heard a crashing sound coming from the staff toilets on the first floor. She went to investigate and found that bottles of cleaning fluids had thrown themselves across the room.

Mr Bower returns

House of Correction (demolished), High Street

One Guildford ghost story had been lost to the annals of history for many years, until recently. It is also one of the town's oldest sightings. There have been several prisons in Guildford's past, all long gone today. The first House of Correction was built along the end of Quarry Street and running up the High Street as far as The Shambles in the early 1600s but no drawings or plans of it – and nothing of its history before 1660 – survive. At the time of the apparition, around 1670, the Master of the House was John Kinge, who had been in position for some years. He can't have been particularly good at his job, or at best was not given funds to do it properly, because when he was dismissed in 1683 the prison was found to be almost ruinous.

The Revd Joseph Glanvill in his *Saducismus Triumphatas* from 1681 recounted the story. It related the sighting of a Mr Bower from Guildford who was found on one of the notoriously dangerous highways just outside the town (this could have been The Mount, Portsmouth Road, London Road or Epsom Road – none of them were safe). His throat had been cut and he had been slashed up the chest as if he were a slaughtered animal. It wasn't long before two suspects were found and placed in the House of Correction along with a recently arrested highwayman who had to share the cell. The highwayman woke in the cell at 1.00 a.m. shortly afterwards and was horrified to see an old man standing in the cell, stooped over and clutching at his back. His throat was cut and a huge gash ran down his front. The ghost made no sound but the highwayman certainly did! On crying out to the pair of suspected murderers, they simply mumbled in their slumbers and turned over.

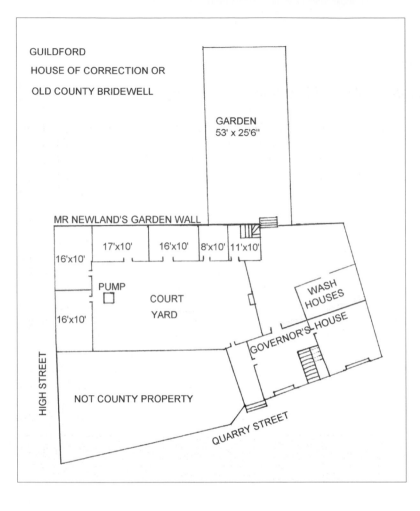

GUILDFORD

HOUSE OF CORRECTION OR

OLD COUNTY BRIDEWELL

GARDEN
53' x 25'6"

MR NEWLAND'S GARDEN WALL

16'x10'

17'x10'   16'x10'   8'x10' 11'x10'

PUMP

COURT

YARD

16'x10'

WASH
HOUSES

GOVERNOR'S HOUSE

HIGH STREET

NOT COUNTY PROPERTY

QUARRY STREET

*A plan of the House
Of Correction in
1822.*

The highwayman's sighting came to the ears of a Mr Reading, a Justice of the Peace and cousin of the murdered man. He met with the prisoner who gave him a detailed account of the ghost. He described the old man's beard, his rough and weathered features and the partial greying of his hair. Apparently, it almost exactly matched Mr Reading's recollections and the prisoner swore an oath he had seen what he claimed (though Glanvill admitted that an oath from a highwayman might not have much value).

Such evidence would be inadmissible at trial but blood had been found on the clothing of one of the men and the other had spoken of the murder two hours before denying he knew one had taken place. Both were duly hanged.

As a postscript, during a period of rebuilding at the back of WHSmith and Waterstone's in the late 1990s the remains of one of the old cells was found, complete with an iron ring for keeping prisoners chained to the walls set into a large block of stone.

Isaac's place

Waterstone's bookshop, No. 50 High Street

A couple of doors up from the junction of the High Street and Quarry Street is Waterstone's bookshop but in 1995 the lower of the two units was a branch of Principles men's clothing. Late one night the manager was awoken by a phone call from the police, asking him to come as soon as possible because all the alarms were going off and they needed him to make sure that no one had broken in and made off with the stock. The manager dragged himself out of bed and remembered he was home alone with his two-year-old son. Of course, he couldn't leave the boy by himself so he gently woke him and put him in the car. On his way out of the house he picked up a pile of stickers which lay by the telephone close to the front door. It was just an afterthought; something for his son to play with inside the building. He arrived at the shop shortly afterwards, greeted by several policemen arranged outside who thanked him for his speed. The manager took the keys from his pocket and they all went in. He and a policeman made their way to the back of the shop where the alarms were kept and he left his son in the company of a WPC, sitting on the stairs. Very quickly the manager established that no one had broken into the shop. No one had even tried. The alarms had simply gone off by themselves. He turned the alarms off and they made their way towards the front of the shop to leave.

On his way out he thanked the WPC for looking after his son but she was quite ashen and said that something had disturbed her. While she was talking to the boy he suddenly stopped replying and then began a conversation over her shoulder into thin air. She asked him whom he was talking to and he said, 'The nice old man behind you'. Apparently this gentleman, invisible to the WPC, was floating 2ft above the ground and then glided out of the shop and down the High Street. However, the manager put this down to his toddler having an imaginary friend. They left again and he turned out the lights and locked the doors, leaving the stickers in a pile on the staircase to clear away the following morning.

When he arrived for work the next day he found in that intervening gap over the rest of the night, someone (or something) had taken each and every sticker from its place on the staircase, peeled it away from its backing and they were now all stuck to the inside of the shop window in a perfect circle.

Early the following year an underground room was discovered here. It was of great age but no one could positively identify what it might have been. Experts came from all over the world and eventually a group from Israel, with historian David Keys, managed to establish that what lay under Waterstone's was a late twelfth-century Jewish scroll-reading room. It is common historical knowledge that England was notoriously anti-Semitic in Medieval times but that Jews had a saving grace in that they were the only people allowed to be money lenders (which could be a double-edged sword when it came to trying to get the money back again). If a Jew wished to practice their faith, it was far safer to do it secretly – and where could be more secret than underground, right at the back of the building?

A moulding in the scroll-reading room does not seem to match any other example in the country – except for one dated to around 1160 in St Mary's church around the corner in Quarry Street. Paint samples taken from the ante-chapel of the castle keep and the room under Waterstone's have proven in laboratory tests to be exactly the same pigment. It is known that at one point there lived in Guildford a rich Jewish merchant called Isaac of Southwark. He had a

Waterstone's bookshop.

house in the High Street. It is recorded his house was damaged by angry anti-Semitic mobs in 1272, three years before the expulsion of the Jews from Royal towns. Is it therefore not possible that this site was once the house of Isaac? If this is plausible is it also not possible that the old man the child was speaking to was Isaac himself? If there is a good chance this is true, could it also not follow that the perfect circle of stickers stuck to the inside window – a circle, I've been informed by a scholar, being a Jewish symbol of goodwill – could have been placed there by none other than Isaac himself, knowing his underground room was about to be discovered and showing that he meant no harm? It is certainly an interesting theory.

Visitors to Waterstone's will be disappointed to learn that the underground room is not open to the public. Since it was discovered the floor level has been lowered. Access is down a ladder and along the length of the shop through little more than a crawl space, which then doubles the entire length back again to reach the room. It is now only 3ft tall and is accessed by a 2ft-high step up into it, the internal measurements being less than 10ft square. Curiously, humidity levels in the chamber have reached an inexplicable 80 per cent – about the same as a sauna.

For some years an interesting photographic mosaic lay over the top of the room and the ground-floor counter was backed by a large glass cabinet displaying all the archaeological finds. In August 2004 the shop went through another refit and Isaac – or whoever still resides there,

The twelfth-century scroll-reading room.

for the building also overlies some of the cells from Guildford's seventeenth-century House Of Correction – came back.

The security guard who worked in the building at night while the renovations were taking place is a practising Muslim. One night he went to the top of the building to pray and as he reached the bottom of the staircase at ground-floor level he was suddenly thrown to the ground by a powerful shove on his shoulders from two hands behind him. He picked himself up and found the building was deserted. He ran out of the building and refused to work there again by himself. The CCTV footage was checked the next morning and indeed he was alone in the shop when it happened.

I was told by the workmen that when they were working on the first floor their hands had been pulled away from the pillars they were painting, they had felt the back of their necks stroked by an unseen hand and had felt circular motions on their scalps. The experiences escalated to such a degree that the management of Waterstone's called in an investigative team from The Ghost Club, headed by myself, to undertake an overnight vigil on the site. On the night of 11 September 2004 the team arrived and paranormal experiences kicked off almost as soon as we started.

Within five minutes of beginning a woman in the team heard a voice on the first floor by the front windows speak in her ear, 'Do you want me?' and then a man on a nearby staircase was hit by a strong but brief smell of roses. A selection of books were taken by the team and placed in a circle on the first floor. These included copies of the Bible, the Koran, the Dead Sea Scrolls and books dealing with the Holocaust and witchcraft. The apparatus in use by the team recorded very high electrical peaks around the circle of books and several members sitting around the circle felt a gust of wind.

On the ground floor the lights flickered, books were seen to ruffle on the shelves and the disabled lift at the back of the shop visibly and audibly banged and rattled twice during the investigation. Two team members were standing close to the front of the shop about 5ft back from the theft alarms that flank the main doors when suddenly they went off of their own volition. Down in the cellar an iron door was heard opening and closing followed by a gurgling noise. Still, one could say, very much a haunted house and certainly one of the more convincing sites I have visited.

The hauntings there continue. Staff have said that Isaac, in various ways, still makes his presence 'felt' on the main staircase. The kettle in the staff room is known to turn itself on and off, the internal phone used to frequently ring with no one there and the main lift has often gone up and down when no one has called it. As late as 30 October 2005 the manageress was in the staff room around 4.00 p.m. when she heard the sound of running water and then a loud, long dragging sound coming from the floor of the nearby staff toilets. She went in to check, as no one was due a tea break and found no trace of anyone nor what had caused the dragging noise. On asking all the staff on the shop floor, none of them had left their positions.

Chapter Two

BEYOND THE HIGH STREET

The Sandemans apparition

Guildford Odeon (demolished), Epsom Road

At the top of Guildford High Street, at the junction with Epsom Road, there is now a modern exclusive penthouse development called Trinity Gate. It stands on the site of the original Guildford Odeon, a large art deco building opened on 13 May 1935, which was demolished in 2002 and has now been replaced by the new multiplex down by the River Wey. In its time not only had the Odeon been Guildford's premier movie-house but in the 1960s groups such as The Beatles and The Rolling Stones had graced its stage (someone is unaware of the fact that John Lennon once played guitar in the space which is now their bathroom).

One of the last films the old cinema ever showed was *First Wives Club* and on 16 November 1996, a man from Dorking by the name of Roy Taylor was sitting watching the film with his girlfriend, Rosemary Crowe. About twenty minutes into the film Roy noticed something strange out of the corner of his eye. He turned to the aisle next to him and was amazed to see a gentleman in a long black cape and wide-brimmed hat pass by him and Rosemary Crowe, walk down past the screen … and straight through it. Roy later described the figure as looking like the logo for Sandemans port.

Roy turned to Rosemary and asked if she'd seen anything. She hadn't, so they continued watching the film. Twenty minutes later, it happened again. The figure in the long black cape and wide-brimmed hat passed by Roy Taylor and Rosemary Crowe, down towards the screen and straight through it. This time Roy turned to Rosemary at the time it was happening and pointed out the figure but still she could see nothing, though she did comment that the air suddenly felt very cold and damp.

As the film neared its end it happened one last time. The figure in the long black cape and wide-brimmed hat passed by them, down towards the screen and straight through it. That was the only time the figure was seen and the cinema was closed shortly afterwards. The current Odeon at the bottom of the town is built on the site of a former sports centre and there have even been strange goings-on there in recent years. Maybe the Sandemans port man enjoys his free films too much to stay put and has decided to move too.

Music hall

The Edinburgh Woollen Mill, Cloth Hall, North Street

At the top of North Street is a curious old-fashioned looking brick building jutting out from a bend in the road. This is a tower built onto Cloth Hall.

Guildford Odeon just prior to demolition in 2001.

The Edinburgh Woollen Mill.

Some years after the Battle of Hastings, a group of Cistercian monks came across to England from Citeaux in France and set up the first Cistercian monastery in Britain at Waverley Abbey near Farnham. Being rather benevolent fellows, at first the lay brothers went out into the local community and on coming to Guildford they taught the locals a trade. They taught them how to work with wool; how to spin it, dye it and sell it. Guildford Blue (as it became known) was shipped all over the known world and was renowned for its high quality and expense. However, by the turn of the seventeenth century the wool trade in Guildford was in decline because the purchasers had found out what the good traders of Guildford used to do. They would stretch the wool so much as it dried on the racks (in Racks Close, just south of the castle) that you only needed to wash it once and it would shrink – so the purchasers took their trade elsewhere.

In 1629 George Abbot built Cloth Hall (originally named The Manufacture) to teach the locals how to work with linen instead of wool. The venture was doomed to failure because within a dozen years the country was at Civil War and people had more important things to think about than what they were going to wear the next day. It was more important to consider where the next meal was coming from, or if you were going to live to see the sunset. There wasn't much call for linen so the building had been converted into four cottages by 1655.

After some years, in the 1670s, the Hall served as the infirmary of the Poor House, a forerunner to what we commonly today call the Workhouse. It was then split into cottages again. It became George Abbot's School in 1855 and in 1861 the tower was added. When the school moved out in 1933 it became offices for the Magistrates Court, becoming a branch of Laura Ashley in the 1970s and at the time of writing it houses the Edinburgh Woollen Mill.

The first hauntings there occurred in the mid-1970s, during the conversion from the offices to the branch of Laura Ashley. Mike Davis, the site foreman, was working with his team of builders one afternoon on the first floor when they heard the sound of a girl crying coming from the empty room above their heads. Then one of the first floor windows – although bolted shut – violently flung itself open. Then things got very unusual indeed. Mike Davis reported to *The Surrey Advertiser*: 'We heard a sound like a trumpet. It came as a straight chord about every ten minutes. It was quite a regular sound'.

This strange sequence of trumpet sounds was heard four or five times over the next nine days. Mike Davis himself had been told that two girls had apparently been murdered in the building. The workmen called in a psychic who spent the night there. She touched the walls, the doors, the ceilings, the floors and gained the aura of the place. The following morning she was able to tell the astonished workmen of her findings. She said that the ghost that haunted the building was that of a young girl, who had been so badly beaten and abused by one of the masters at the time when it had been used as a Victorian school that she had died as a result of her injuries. This was very chilling and convincing … until Mike Davis found out this had been a boys' school!

The next haunting there occurred in 1979. By now the branch of Laura Ashley was up and running. Two Saturday girls, by the names of Sharon Bryant and Julie Butcher, worked there. One afternoon both girls were working in the stockroom (which was always unusually cold) when they suddenly heard three loud raps on the window. Somebody on the street outside playing a prank, one might think – but in 1979 the stockroom was on the top floor. Both girls suddenly had a feeling they were being watched and ran downstairs rather quickly. Then things began to heat up.

On coming into work some mornings members of staff would see a vague mist floating around the stockroom floor which would slowly disappear before their eyes. On one occasion Sharon saw this for herself, then heard the sound of heavy breathing behind her and ran downstairs rather quickly. Some mornings the staff would hear the sounds of conversation above their heads in the empty building and the cleaner refused to work there at night, saying she was disturbed by the sound of a young girl singing coming from the top floor.

In May 2003 I was told by a member of staff that one day she had been working behind the counter on the ground floor of the tower when she noticed that the normal traffic sounds from outside had disappeared. She then heard a horse and coach hurtling up North Street towards the building so she looked out of the window, surprised to see nothing that could explain the noises. As she continued to look out for this anachronism, the sound of the horse and coaches went straight past the building and up towards Chertsey Street but she had seen nothing to account for it.

The most recent event was at the end of 2005 when Janet Drake, who had worked in the building for some years knowing all about the ghosts but never experiencing anything herself, went up to the first floor. It was the middle of the afternoon and as she entered the menswear section she heard something over the sound of the piped music. It was a sudden short sound of children laughing which immediately cut dead when she came into the room. Janet joked that she felt maybe she had 'caught them' by walking in so quickly. She says there is never any kind of bad atmosphere in the building but many of the staff say that the first floor can feel odd at times.

Bloody cellar

The Live and Let Live, No. 57 Haydon Place

There are two pubs in Guildford for which I have a soft spot. They are pubs that have retained an old appearance but more importantly do not have loud, blaring music and loud, blaring customers. One of those is the Three Pigeons and the other is one of Guildford's better kept secrets, the Live and Let Live that stands almost by itself at the end of Haydon Place off the top of North Street. Even walking up to the building you see a banner along its side wall saying 'Enjoy a drink with some real spirits'. Inside you find a friendly welcome from the staff and customers, usually a few of the local 'old boys'. The pub has certainly not shied away from its supernatural activity; in fact it has embraced it and uses it as a valuable marketing tool. I first became aware of it having any ghosts when it took out an advertisement in the local paper.

It is one of the newer 'old' pubs in Guildford and was opened in the 1860s, although its time of construction could have been up to thirty years before that date. A butcher, named John Stapleton, sold the plot of land, then called Church Acre, to the Farnham brewer John Trimmer in February 1864. By 1868 the house, which included a woodshed and a well, had been opened as the Live and Let Live by the occupant, a man named Bird.

A previous landlord had recounted once seeing a ghostly man in the corner of the small bar but things took a more active turn with the arrival of the current landlady Julia MacDiarmid at the turn of the third Millennium. After closing one night in 2000 several of the staff stayed behind chatting at the bar and then suddenly they all heard banging feet running up the cellar steps towards them. Apparently, one of the staff's hair literally stood on end. They waited for the door handle to turn but nothing happened. The staff that didn't live there quickly made their excuses and left.

The cellar consists of two small rooms separated by a large door. About a year later Julia was down there and turned some of the barrels off but within a couple of minutes, they had turned themselves back on again. At the end of 2005 the reverse happened when gas taps in the cellar started turning themselves off. This happened to two of the taps and on one occasion it happened twice within a few moments.

In the summer of 2005 Julia had been outside in the tiny garden when she glanced up at the flat above. She momentarily caught a glimpse of a boy with blond hair looking out of the kitchen window. This window is directly over a sink and there is no way a child could have got that close to the glass. Julia's two sons (neither of them blond, I must quickly add) have lived in the building with her for seven years. In all of that time, they have only ever spent half a night in the back bedroom, claiming that the odd atmosphere in the room makes them feel uncomfortable.

Curious to understand better what may have happened at the building and with an interest in the paranormal, Julia requested an investigation by a local ghost-hunting group who spent a night in the pub in February 2005. Their report is very detailed and includes both interesting events and some assumptions that have no basis in fact.

The team captured many orbs on their cameras and on video over the vigil but they rightly concede these may well be dust or insects. One of the team saw a shadow in a corner of the

The Live and Let Live.

cellar. During the night a gas tap turned itself off and one of the heavy barrels jammed in between two others rumbled as it moved by itself. Loose wires by the cellar door waved as if being blown by a wind. A medium in the group is reported to have told the other team members that the lights in the cellar would go out after she left, which apparently happened. A rubber mallet being used as a 'control object' (an inanimate object placed on a surface to see if it moves) shifted half an inch just after midnight. This may not sound impressive but half an inch with no visible means of moving it is intriguing, presuming it wasn't nudged by one of the team by accident. One of the bedrooms was very cold all evening. A ball of light whizzed across one of the beams in the bar but there appeared to be nothing to cause it.

The mediums in the group also sensed some remarkable events and people throughout the investigation but almost all of their psychic findings can be dismissed. Firstly, there was a supposition this had once been a thriving and busy part of town with stables but Haydon Place was always a back road. Secondly, they also felt the building used to be much larger, the cellar steps used to be in a different position and part of the building was once hit by a bomb or bulldozed, but there is nothing to back this up.

Unfortunately, the real issues arise when reading the mediums' accounts of the people who once lived here. The extended family consisted of a butcher called George Burrows, his wife Elizabeth, their four children and George's seventy-five-year-old mother Martha who died of pneumonia. George had beaten and abused his children in the bedroom at the back of the building and as a result of this, Elizabeth had killed him with a cleaver in the cellar in 1865. For this, she was arrested and hanged in Guildford. Needless to say, not only is there not a shred of evidence any of these people ever existed but also executions in Guildford had ceased around a century before. By this stage Surrey criminals were being hanged in London. They also sensed a Victorian policeman standing outside the pub and a woman in black clothing nearby. As one of the mediums recalled the hanging, he felt something tightening around his throat.

The mediums also claimed to have picked up other entities in the building, such as a murderer who had been hanged at Tyburn (Marble Arch as it is today) which had followed the landlady from her previous job. He had apparently tormented his victim by lying on top of her as she got into bed and on the night of the investigation, his spirit had invaded the body of one of the team. They also sensed a woman called Bernadette who entered several of the team members and a heavily pregnant woman who had fallen down the stairs which had caused her no injuries but natural concern for the baby's well-being.

Such tales are frequently 'sensed' by mediums in haunted buildings and I have never once encountered a case where this could be validated by documentary evidence. To use the excuse 'that doesn't prove it never happened' just doesn't wash, especially when we are talking about extreme murder cases. In spite of these unlikely stories there is every possibility that the Live and Let Live is a building with, at least, a poltergeist and long may it continue.

Lorna – the most prolific ghost in Guildford

Sydenham Road and Tunsgate

She might not be the most famous ghost in the town (though not far off) but boy, does she get about! There are not many ghosts who can claim they haunt at least four buildings in three streets – and, if some are to be believed, died in two different places.

The legend – for legend it must remain, as there are no records to back up the tale – begins like this. In the closing years of the 1600s, shortly after the purchase of the first Quaker property in Guildford in North Street in 1673, a rich Quaker lived in a large house which is now occupied by Sydenham Road car park, right next to Holy Trinity church. This at least is fairly likely for although by the Victorian era this was mostly a field, on the town ichnography of 1739 there were indeed many houses on this patch of land separated by an area of parkland. With this widower was his eldest daughter of nineteen, who was named Lorna. The location of this house will never really be known but many photographs exist of the Queen's Head pub which stood directly next to the back of Holy Trinity church in Sydenham Road until its demolition for the car park in 1959. It has been suggested it was a pub from the 1500s but no records survive to confirm this. It was certainly in use as a pub called the Bell and Trumpet as early as 1701 when a traveller from Cornwall died while staying there. Could this just possibly have been the house where Lorna lived? Photographs show an uneven old building almost entirely hung with curved tiles, with a jettied first floor and a large garret room gabled out of the middle of the roof. Or maybe it was the whitewashed building next door, also clearly seen on old photographs?

So the stories say, the family was one of the first to join the Quaker movement in Guildford. At that time Sydenham Road was called South Street. Lorna, being young and attractive, had been courting a local young man of whom her father disapproved. The reason? He was an Anglican who refused Lorna's father's demands that if ever he were to become part of the family

South Street. (David Rose collection)

Racks Close in the 1920s.

Tunsgate Baptist Chapel in the early 1950s. (Margaret Brady)

he too should become a Quaker. In one final attempt to bring the lad to heel, at Christmas one year he was invited for a meal at the house. Unfortunately, not being a typical Quaker, and certainly not full of Christmas cheer, during the evening Lorna's father started to question her boyfriend quite intently about his background, family, prospects and, more and more pressingly, his religious inclinations.

Eventually, Lorna's father went too far. The boy snapped back at him and a shouting match began. He stormed out of the building, leaving Lorna utterly distraught with a father brimming with self-righteous rage. We can only guess at the scene which followed within the house but can expect it would have included a seventeenth-century version of such classic lines as, 'I wish I'd never been born!' Lorna was a broken girl. In fury and tears, she grabbed her mop-cap and ran off into the dark of winter. By the time he retired, Lorna's father had not witnessed his daughter returning. Maybe she had caught up with her boyfriend and was with him.

This was, in fact, not the case. When daylight came, Lorna was discovered lying at the bottom of the cliff at nearby Racks Close, just beyond the castle and on the town boundary. In her despair, she had stumbled over the edge the previous night and had been lying there in the freezing weather for hours with many broken bones. She was taken back to her father's house where later that day she died from exposure and internal injuries. The story continues that Lorna's father was so hard-hearted he refused to allow her to be buried in the family plot in Quaker's Acre (on the south side of North Street, opposite the Friends' Meeting House).

Reports of a lady in grey around this area began in the early Victorian years but as time went on they diminished until the sightings were lost to history. In 1860, on the corner of Castle Square just yards away from the site of the old house, the Baptist Chapel was built. It seated 200 and was made of brick. The threat of demolition began in 1937 and in 1954, as part of the redevelopment of Tunsgate that had previously been a narrow and slum-like alleyway, it was finally pulled down. Obviously, to prevent any accidents, Tunsgate and that part of Castle Street were closed to traffic and pedestrians while the building was torn down. Imagine, then, the amazement of a bulldozer driver when – as the rubble fell – he noticed a young woman with long golden hair and blue eyes, wearing a long grey dress walk out of the rubble now covering the old burial ground to the north of the chapel. She then, completely ignoring him and the demolition work, walked straight down Tunsgate and into a shop near the bottom on the right-hand side.

This sighting too was eventually forgotten but the stories began again in the 1970s. The shop in question is No. 15 Tunsgate and at that time it was a florist's. An employee saw a woman enter the shop and walk up the staircase but no one came back down. In the 1980s the shop was a branch of Monsoon clothing. A shop assistant was on the shop floor by herself while the manageress was taking a break in the staff room when she noticed a young woman in a grey dress ignore her when entering the shop and walk straight up the stairs to the showroom on the first floor. Being the only member of staff on duty she followed her but when she got to the top of the stairs she found it was deserted. She looked beyond the doors, back downstairs and out into the street but there was no sign of the lady in the grey dress. Now very concerned she ran in to the manageress and blurted out what had just happened. Her boss's reply was a calm, 'Ah, you've just seen the ghost, haven't you? Sorry – we did think of telling you about her but we thought it might scare you'. Nothing has been seen in the shop for some years now but the staff do occasionally hear noises in the building that they can't explain.

But Lorna doesn't stop at these two sites. Construction on the (now demolished and rebuilt) Sydenham Road car park began in 1962 and took seven years to complete. It is interesting to note that the far nicer car park that replaced it only took about eighteen months to build. In the

Number 15 Tunsgate.

final stages of completion in late 1969 two workmen were painting pillars and barriers on the first floor. Though the building was not yet ready to allow the public inside, they saw a young woman in a long grey dress with golden hair under a black mop-cap standing at the far end of the floor. On calling out to her she turned to face them. She had a thin face and was beautiful but looked in total despair. Thinking they had encountered a possible suicide, the men started to walk towards her but as they did so she simply faded away like a mist before their eyes. It is supposed that she had been standing where her bedroom had once been.

This part of the tale has been recounted in many books over the years. Most of the versions mention Sydenham Road car park but a few claim this story concerns York Road car park half a mile away. York Road car park is built in part of an old chalk quarry and the theory is that the ghost is seen where she died rather than where she lived. A Guildford woman who had heard the story used to go to the area and speak to her, sensing she was there but never seeing or hearing anything. In the end you pay your money and take your choice but my reasoning is this: I do not believe York Road car park is the site because to get there, Lorna would have had to cross through the town and not only would she have been seen but primitive psychology dictates that she wouldn't want to be seen in hysterics by other people. The chalk cliff at Racks Close is much closer than the chalk pit at Foxenden Quarry and she would not have had to pass other buildings to get there. Finally, why would she be seen standing in the middle of a car park which during her lifetime would have been thin air?

Even today, teams of paranormal investigators have staked out the car park in Sydenham Road in the hope of catching something unusual but Lorna has not been seen or heard for many years on this spot. She has moved a few yards to the west, back in the direction of Tunsgate. In 2003 a woman on my ghost tour had told me that she had been walking along the alleyway called Milkhouse Gate which adjoins the car park some years previously and was stunned to see a young woman in a long grey dress walk right through the wall in front of her and immediately disappear through the wall on the other side. About six months after this I spoke to a young man who told me he had passed the end of Milkhouse Gate one evening and saw a young woman in a grey dress standing at the Sydenham Road end who had then begun to walk down the alleyway before disappearing.

Lorna is not the only ghost at Sydenham Road car park. During the long building period of the 1960s various locals when passing the site at night had seen what they took to be a nun floating through the area. The churches jumped on board. The Anglican Church yelled, 'It's a Protestant nun!' The Catholic Church cried, 'No! It's a Catholic nun!' The only way both parties could be placated was when two separate exorcisms were held on the site to stop the hauntings. Someone told me, quite seriously, that one person had died of fright after seeing the ghost of the nun. This piece of information has no basis in fact at all of which I'm aware. However, in spite of psychics visiting the area and claiming they have led her to peace, Lorna is still in the area and is still very active.

Ghosts go downstairs, daddy

Guildford Castle, Castle Street

The impressive Norman tower of Guildford Castle is one of the oldest standing structures in Surrey. The origins of the fortification date back to the years immediately following the Battle of Hastings. There was a wooden stockade surrounded by a defensive barrier with barracks and stables for soldiers in place here no later than 1071. All that remains of the original castle is the earth mound upon which the current keep sits. Suggestions as to the date of this building vary greatly and as research progresses those views are bound to change again. At the time of writing, current opinion places it in the first half of the twelfth century. During a massive period of renovation in 2003 – in which floors and a roof were reinstated for the first time in 400 years – the conservators found it had been built in two stages, which explains why the structure is now rendered up to a point where battlements are marked out below the modern-day roof level.

Guildford Castle Keep (or the Great Tower as it was known in antiquity) stood as the County Prison for Surrey and Sussex for 300 years until Sussex prisoners were moved to Lewes Castle in 1347 and the remaining Surrey prisoners to the Marshalsea in London, around 1500. Many of the individuals held in the keep were accused of murder and the prison was simply a means of keeping people confined until the Magistrates Court came to town. If an individual was found innocent at trial they were released. If, however, they were found guilty then they would return overnight to the castle and usually the following day would be executed.

Curiously, given its dark history, there are precious few ghost stories connected to the castle – although that number is growing – and none of these tales pre-date the 1950s.

*The Great Tower,
Guildford Castle.*

During one period of renovation, in 1951, the workmen were informed by a local that the tower was haunted by the spirit of a young woman who was periodically seen on the spiral staircase that leads to the roof, not knowing whether or not she should go up or down the stairs. Guildford Castle is unusual in that its staircase runs anti-clockwise. Most castle keeps run the other way. The iron staircase today dates from 1888 and some have suggested the ghost is lost because the direction of the staircase has changed. This is entirely erroneous, however, as not only are the marks of the original stone staircase still clear at points but if that staircase had run in the other direction, then the entrance and exits could not be where they are.

I have been Senior Custodian of the building for Guildford Borough Council since 1994 and before we shut for the renovation work in 2000 the ticket booth was a small hole carved into the 11ft thick walls. In that kiosk the staff member would have no idea what was happening inside the building. In the few years leading up to the closure an event would happen late each season, always in late August or early September. A young mother would visit the keep in the company of their young son or daughter who would be between three and five years old. No sooner would they go into the keep and down the stairs to the ground floor that acted as the

*The haunted corner of the
ground floor of the castle.*

prison than the mother would reappear, the child in near hysterics. The flustered parent would apologise to me as they left: 'I'm sorry, she couldn't stand it in there. She says she was scared by the man chained up to the walls at the bottom'. Not only was this the correct location but records show that on many occasions fetters were ordered so the prisoners could be chained up to the walls. The fact that the east and west walls are still complete but that both the north and south walls have been largely robbed of stone to a height of 2ft suggests that maybe these once held worked stone into which the fetters would have been rooted.

In July 2005 a teenage girl visited the keep. She told the staff member she was psychic and could see a man dressed like a monk who was chained up in the north-east corner of the ground floor. She then went upstairs but only got halfway to the roof before she returned, saying she couldn't go all the way up as 'something' was blocking her way.

On 13 November 2005 (the last day of the season which was coincidentally Remembrance Sunday) at 1.30 p.m., a gentleman visited the keep with his wife and two young sons shortly after the service had been held at the War Memorial in the castle grounds. At about 1.45 p.m. the father was standing in the cage on the roof with his elder son (aged about six) and they were both looking out over the town centre. Out of the corner of his eye, he saw his younger son (about three years old) standing next to him. He looked out over the town again and then turned to speak to the youngest boy. To his concern, he found the child was no longer on the roof at all. Understandably worried his toddler son had tried to negotiate the many spiral steps back down by himself the father ran down the staircase to intercept him, only to find that there was no one on it. In fact, his wife and younger son were still on the first floor and were only just beginning to ascend the stairs. As soon as the father reached them the child said, without any prompting, the curious sentence, 'Ghosts go downstairs, daddy'.

In the 1980s a member of Guildford Borough Council staff, entrusted with the task of locking the gardens up in the evening, was annoyed to see a member of the public on top of the castle motte in the lower gardens, which he had just inspected and locked up. She was looking out towards him and was dressed in what the employee took to be a rather eccentric manner. She seemed to be wearing what he could only describe as being an old-fashioned Victorian dress. He unlocked the gates again and ran up the motte to ask her to leave but when he got there he found it was deserted and the woman was nowhere to be seen. The sighting may be unrelated but this could possibly have a connection with the haunting at Guildford Museum just outside the gardens.

Ironically, I have probably spent more time in Guildford Castle Keep than anyone alive today and in spite of this I have never personally witnessed anything unusual in all my time there.

A good neck for music

Guildford Museum, Quarry Street

Guildford Museum is a strange hotchpotch of several buildings and dates, in a way that a museum should be. A section of the building is built onto Castle Arch, built by John of Gloucester (Henry III's Master Mason) in 1256 as the entrance to Guildford Castle after much of the palace was destroyed in a fire two years before. The south side of the building dates from the early 1600s and is a Jacobean winged hall built by the Carter family, who quite possibly had just given up on the idea of living in the old castle keep. The single storey entrance on Quarry Street is comparatively recent, being added to the rest of the building in 1911.

During the late Victorian years many people used to see the hazy shape of a woman who entered the building through the back, via the castle grounds. Shortly after this, they would hear the sound of a piano playing coming from the top floor of No. 48 Quarry Street, which is now part of the museum. People would scratch their heads, wondering what the cause could be – then some bright spark remembered the scandal of a few years before when No. 48 had been a girls' school. The music teacher in a fit of depression had hanged herself in the music room … on the top floor at the front of the building.

The story passed into legend but came back with a vengeance in 1990. By this time the caretaker of the museum was a man called Peter and he and his wife had a guest to stay with them in the caretaker's grace and favour flat, which occupies the first floor of No. 48. They were put in the guestroom and the following morning over breakfast Peter asked if their visitor had had a good night's sleep. The said they hadn't and were asked why. They replied they had been kept awake all night by the sound of someone playing a piano coming from the room upstairs.

This was far from the last time the piano-playing ghost was heard. Later that same year one of the staff was working on the top floor but in an office at the back when they too heard

Above: *Guildford Museum in the 1930s.*

Right: *The staircase in No. 48 Quarry Street.*

the sound of the supernatural musician. He opened the window to gauge where the sound was coming from but as soon as he did so, it stopped. He closed it and the music began again, opened it and it stopped. He closed the window one last time and let the music play on until it gradually faded away. He told me the music he'd heard was a well-known classical piece but he had no idea of its name. Another museum colleague was working in the same back office on a different occasion and he also heard the sound of the piano. He was able to identify it as one of Chopin's *Impromptus* – a piece which would have been quite popular in the second half of the nineteenth century.

A female employee now works in the office where the tragedy is alleged to have happened. Although it is on the top floor, at 2.00 p.m. one afternoon she heard a huge thud come from the ceiling in the room which she could not explain. All three employees that work on the top floor have been present on many occasions when they have heard someone running up the steep, narrow staircase to their offices – but whenever they have looked out onto the landing to see who has arrived, it is often deserted.

On one occasion in the 1990s, Peter the caretaker was away from the flat on business and his wife was alone in the bedroom. She heard the sound of someone entering the building from the ground floor, up the stairs to the caretaker's flat and then enter. The feet walked up to the bedroom door and the door handle began to turn. The door then opened 6 inches before closing again and the feet walked back out of the flat. A few moments later, the familiar sound of the running feet was heard going up to the top floor. Alfie, the current caretaker, has sometimes heard the sound of thuds and bangs in the early hours of the morning but nothing worse than that.

This is not the only occurrence in Guildford Museum, however. The main body of the building has its fair share of paranormal phenomena too. For years the staff have commented on the sounds of feet running up and down the main staircase in Castle Arch, muffled voices from empty rooms and feeling someone with them as they open up in the morning. They certainly don't like going down into the cellar that lies next to the old archway.

Such an aversion was found to be vindicated, for in the year 2000 a male employee entered this cellar and was dumbfounded to see what he took to be a bag of flour being flung about. This then solidified into the shape of a woman which walked straight past him, into the north-east corner of the room and then passed straight through the solid wall which had once been a staircase leading up through the building and has been blocked for more than 200 years.

In October 2002 during one of my Ghost Tours a member of the group spent the entire time outside the museum staring through the windows at the CCTV screens, his hands cupped around his face and seemingly ignoring the unfolding stories. As I knew the gentleman concerned I spent some time talking to him once the walk had finished and he said, 'I hope you don't think I was being rude at the museum. I wasn't ignoring you – I was just fascinated by what was going on behind you'. I had been standing on the top step of the main doorway. Although the museum was dark inside and had been empty for four hours I was told that an umbrella had lifted itself out of the umbrella stand behind the door and was dancing around of its own volition directly behind me.

In 2005 an elderly gentleman visited the museum and told us he had been one of the builders contracted to work on refurbishment there in the early 1950s. He claimed that the partial skeletal remains of a man and child were unearthed here at that time. This may well be a mistake on his part, judgement clouded by time, but he seemed very sure of his story.

*The haunted cellar in
Castle Arch.*

The house-swapping lady in white

Rosemary Alley, Quarry Street

The name, Rosemary Alley, opposite the junction of Quarry Street and Castle Street, conjures up lovely images: an English country garden; home cooking; aromatherapy... Even the present site bears witness to this romance, a narrow little alleyway overhung with jettied Tudor buildings (although the façades are Georgian), sensitive lighting and little sets of steps rhythmically cascading down to the River Wey beyond. But it was not always so. Rosemary Alley is a 'false' Victorian name. The alleyway's original title was Pisspot Alley; the reason being it was an open running sewer full of effluence, slops, rainwater and rats. You can see why they changed the name, but I must say it would look wonderful on a modern map of Guildford.

For many years an unidentified lady in white haunted the buildings on either side (No. 8 to the south and No. 6 to the north). Apparently she used to float from the first floor of No. 8

and – not having been seen in the gap of Rosemary Alley – reappear in No. 6. Her frequent appearances so scared the cleaner in one of the buildings that a blessing was held to remove the ghost. Which building that was is not recorded but it was likely to be No. 8, as No. 6 has witnessed phenomena in recent history. In September 1995 workmen were carrying out subsidence repairs to the building and found what they called 'a hot spot' on the ground floor. A single floorboard was inexplicably found to be too hot to stand on, yet the floorboards either side of it and those above and below were always found to be perfectly cool. A strange inversion from the usual cold spots associated with hauntings unless, of course, the rest of the building was so haunted that this floorboard was the only clear area – but that is hardly likely.

On speaking to the staff in both buildings, most of the employees had never heard of the ghost but a gentleman in No. 8 said, 'Yes, we were haunted once but we're not now' and didn't seem keen to discuss it further.

As an aside, at the bottom of Rosemary Alley behind No. 6, now fronting Millbrook, is part of the Founders Studio used by the Guildford Conservatoire (formerly the more pronounceable Guildford School of Acting). I suspect none of the drama students are aware they rehearse for their musicals on the site of Guildford's mortuary from 1904. It was demolished in the mid-1960s. Before the construction of Millbrook in 1961 it had stood at the end of a dead-end (quite literally) lane. Fronting a busy thoroughfare to the south is not such a good location for a mortuary.

The most haunted pub in Guildford

The King's Head pub, Quarry Street

The King's Head used to be in the building on the north side of the junction of Quarry Street and Castle Street but by the end of the eighteenth century it was found to be getting too small and so two seventeenth-century cottages on the other side of the junction were knocked through into one and the pub has remained there ever since. During the Second World War a Canadian soldier was shot outside the pub by a local man with whose wife, it is said, he was having an affair. Whether he has anything to do with the strange goings-on inside is quite another matter.

In the 1980s the landlords of The King's Head came and went with alarming regularity. In 1985 the outgoing landlord told the incoming one he thought there was something unusual about the pub. He felt that perhaps it might be haunted. The head barman who'd been there for some years laughed. He said he'd never found anything unusual but two years later he was to eat those words. When calling time at the bar at 11 o'clock one night he suddenly froze. One of the locals asked him what was wrong and he replied, 'She's over there by the beam! Can't you see her?' but the locals could see nothing.

When they'd managed to calm him down he told them he'd seen an old lady standing by the bar staring back at him, grey and indistinct. Shortly after this, one of the internal doors flung itself violently open and the pub dog went berserk. The dog was then seen on many occasions sitting on the floor, barking at a spot in the wall where a blocked-up doorway once led down into the cellar.

In the cellar itself a lone female voice has been known to call members of staff by name but whenever they get to the bottom of the cellar steps they always find it deserted. A man has

The King's Head.

reputedly been spotted in the pub reading a newspaper but disappears when approached. Just recently the pub has acquired a new ghost. A little girl, wearing a white lace Victorian dress has been seen on numerous occasions standing just inside the doorway before skipping through the pub and disappearing through the French windows at the back. She has been seen so frequently the staff have given her a name – Mary.

In August 2002 I had a large group of about seventy people with me on the Ghost Tour. At that time, I used to stand on the steps of the pub itself. The group was so large that a woman in the group was standing next to me on the top step. As soon as I mentioned Mary's name the lady jumped off the step, almost into the arms of the man standing below. I thought she was having a joke but at the end of the evening, she confided to me that as soon as I'd mentioned Mary's name she'd actually felt a cold, small hand push her leg out of the way.

A few weeks later myself and John Fraser (a colleague from The Ghost Club) were interviewed at the pub for a Japanese television documentary about ghosts in Britain. Around this time I approached the landlord to arrange an overnight investigation at the site. He was working on the pub's PA system in the beer garden at the back while I was talking to him. The second I broached the subject of an investigation, one of the speakers blew. This may simply be a coincidence but there is a legend connected with the pub that says if ever there is any unpleasantness inside, the plumbing and electrics will start to break down. At no point was this more evident than in February 1995, when overnight the ceiling of the pub caved in, due in no small part to the poor foundations of the structure and an infestation of deathwatch beetle. It has been suggested this may have been the north-west corner of the curtain wall of the castle. Archaeologists moved in,

The cellar in the King's Head.

finding a medieval building underneath and proof it had once been used as a cobbler's shop (this may explain the 'cobblers' you can hear as you pass the building any Friday night). The repair work took far longer to carry out than the workmen intended, however. Every time they started their machinery it would break down. They would take items out onto the street or into the beer garden and everything would be working perfectly, only to break down again once they got it back inside.

And so that is where the tale would have ended, had I not met a psychic who once worked there. She claims that there are, in fact, only two ghosts at the pub – and they are Mary and the woman in the cellar. Contrary to what the other staff members have said, she maintains that Mary is not a Victorian child at all but a small, scruffy woman aged about thirty who was a servant in one of the cottages prior to the conversion into a pub and suffered a violent death after being pushed into one of the fireplaces. Apparently Mary sometimes wears her hair pulled back, which makes her look like a child and she hates men. The ex-employee has seen windows opening and closing and large, heavy ashtrays moving about. One night she found several bar stools in the middle of the street at 2.00 a.m. Another night she woke up to find the blankets were being held over her head and as she managed to pull them away she was hit by a vision of the downstairs of the pub as it had looked hundreds of years before. Mary has been known to process food orders on the electronic system in the pub, which get sent through to upstairs, even though the pub has been closed.

To counteract all this trouble, it appears the woman in the cellar is more helpful. It seems she keeps an eye on the beer pumps and has been known to shout such things as, 'Fosters off!' just as the barrels are at the point of running dry!

Where the dead come back — sometimes

St Mary's church, Quarry Street and The Mount

The tower of St Mary's church in Quarry Street is the oldest standing building in Guildford. It is actually Saxon, dating back to the year 1050. It probably acted as the Royal Church in Guildford. It is known the body of Prince Henry lay here in 1274 before being taken for burial at Westminster Abbey and wall paintings uncovered in 1825 (now lost) have been attributed to William Florentine. Henry III employed him for decorating parts of Guildford Palace. The bells of St Mary's would be tolling every night before an execution was due to be held here. They would still be tolling the next day when the condemned were taken from their holding place in the castle keep, on the back of a cart along Quarry Street and then up to The Mount where they'd meet their maker. Under an Act of King Henry VIII, condemned murderers were to be given after their deaths to the medical schools, so the students could cut them up and see how the human body worked. Members of the public also often attended such activities. This allowance was stopped by the Anatomy Act of 1830 and only became acceptable again recently with Professor Gunther Von Hagens' Bodyworlds exhibition and public autopsy in the East End of London and on television.

Because there was now a shortage of bodies this gave rise to the likes of Burke and Hare in Edinburgh. Bodysnatching was known throughout the country and Guildford wasn't to escape the scare. It became very popular to rent (or if you were rich, to buy) an extremely heavy coffin-shaped slab, six or seven inches thick and made of solid stone to rest over your tomb until your body had rotted away enough to be of no further use to science. The weight of such an obstruction would mean that any prospective 'resurrectionist' would need a gang of half a dozen men to make any leeway into the grave. There are several examples of these stones still extant on the south side of the church.

By the 1850s the graveyard was getting overcrowded. Body was buried on top of body and by the middle of the decade bodies were buried so close to the surface that it only took a few heavy rainstorms and they'd start to come back. Rotting skulls appearing through the topsoil ... fingertips turning up in people's drinking water supplies ... decomposing legs gently bobbing down the River Wey. Well, maybe not the last one — but gruesomely, certainly the first and very possibly the second! The smell passing by the church in summer was said to be awful. Locals passing at night were convinced it was haunted, as they would see flickering lights above newly-filled graves. We now know better. These are almost certainly will-o'-the-wisps, self-igniting methane gas caused by decomposing flesh. In 1860 all the town centre cemeteries were technically closed and from then on burials were held in the Mount Cemetery, opened in 1856 and where the author Charles Lutwidge Dodgeson (better known as Lewis Carroll) who died in Guildford in 1898 is buried.

A rare image of St Mary's church in the late 1860s.

There was one final funeral service held here. On the northern side of the town centre is The Friary shopping centre. It's called The Friary because it is built on top of a thirteenth-century Dominican friary. Eleanor of Provence chose the site in memory of her six-year-old grandson Prince Henry who had died at Guildford Castle on 20 October 1274. When construction began on the shopping centre exactly 700 years later, the workmen and archaeologists found the foundations of the friary church beneath and by 1978 had uncovered the bones of sixty-five individuals who had been buried there – some of whom had died from the Plague. It's not thought to be 'proper' to build a mass of shops on top of graves and so the bones were exhumed and given to the Ancient Monuments Laboratory. They dated them, analysed them and having no further use for them gave them back to Guildford Museum who sat for many years on box upon box of mouldering skeletons in the cellar. Not a very fitting end.

In 1987 the curator of the museum, Matthew Alexander, gained permission from the vicar of St Mary's – who in turn had to gain permission from the Queen herself – to hold one final funeral service here. Mr Alexander constructed a large custom-made coffin. He made the dimensions just right to bury the sixty-five sets of remains held in the museum. The bones of all the people who had been buried there were deposited within it and with due ceremony on 26 September they were buried just to the right of the main gateway which today is marked by a lavender bed. However, no one had taken into account how heavy dozens of skeletons might be and the weight was so excessive that the burial ceremony began with the coffin being hauled along Quarry Street on a trolley. A small stone plaque in the nearby wall, which has had the date recarved due to an initial error by the stonemason, is – beyond a few finds and an impressive lead coffin now in show in the museum – the only other reminder the friars were ever in Guildford at all. It's ironic that time ran out for the archaeologists and most of the graves of the actual friars – who it is suspected were buried under the cloister – now lie beneath the shops.

The Mount Cemetery.

Going back to The Mount for a moment, this cemetery stands at the end of a very steep hill seen on the other side of the river from the High Street but fundamentally the same road. Before the building of the Hog's Back this was the main road into Guildford from the west. The approach was so steep that local boys would wait at the top of the hill so they could be paid for acting as brakes by hanging onto the backs of the coaches as they descended to the town. Likewise, extra horses were kept at the bottom of The Mount to enable those same carriages to go back up again. Beyond the Mount Cemetery, that vital road is now only a footpath.

The Mount cemetery was initially constructed around the area of Booker's Tower – essentially a folly erected by Charles Booker, three times a Mayor of Guildford, in 1839 in memory of his two teenage sons who both died tragically. Several members of Guildford Borough Council staff have opened the cemetery gates in the morning – especially on misty days – to see a man already inside, walking his dog amongst the tombstones. Each time he suddenly disappears.

It was further along The Mount on the open part of the hill close to the comparatively modern Farnham Road, where the majority of Guildford's executions were held, certainly in the eighteenth century. It may well have hosted some of Guildford's disposal of those accused of witchcraft in the sixteenth century. These trials were held at the Guildhall and included tragic tales of what we would regard simply as childminders being able to take insufficient care of their charges. One account refers to a baby falling out of the arms of its carer and dropping into a fire. For this 'pact with Satan' the unfortunate woman in whose trust the baby had been left was hanged as a witch. Guildford's final witchcraft trial was held in 1701 and resulted in the man who brought the charges, Richard Hathaway, being whipped through the High Street for perjury. Defoe refers to the executions in his *Tour Through Great Britain* published in the 1720s. All the executions held on The Mount were straightforward hangings. The actual execution spot is believed to be in the vicinity of a small tree halfway up the hill next to the path from the end of the Wodeland Avenue and Farnham Road junction. It is said that the executions were held there so that businessmen who had shops in the High Street didn't have to shut up shop for the day to join the 'celebrations' around the scaffold. They could stand at their doorways, watch the man die and then get back to work. However, the execution spot is about a mile from the top of the High Street making it very difficult to see what was going on. This distant view was as good as the shopkeepers would get because repeat performances were sadly rarely scheduled.

Noisy neighbours
The Star, No. 2 Quarry Street

The Star stands on the corner of Quarry Street where it joins to the lower edge of the High Street and until the construction of Millbrook in 1961, this road was the route to Brighton. It was known as Star Corner for many years and some old locals still know it as such. The assumption is that John Child (three-time Mayor of Guildford) bought the Star in 1684 but there are no references to it prior to 1723. It changed hands about half a dozen times throughout the rest of the eighteenth century. In 1833 one of the owners, a Jesse Boxall, left the Star to become Master at Abbot's Hospital but by the end of the Victorian era the pub was still in family ownership. A curious anomaly about the Star is that the passageway leading to the toilets is said to this day to be a right of way for drovers taking their sheep to market.

The pub closed for renovations for about a year in 1972 and it now houses three bars. Although the Star's main ghost story is undated, it is said it happened 'in the early seventies'. It is fairly safe to assume, given all the poltergeist activity that seems to take place during times that building work is being undertaken, that it occurred shortly before or after the renovations took place. At about 2.00 a.m. the landlord and his wife woke up with a start to hear the sound of barrels crashing and smashing together in the cellar. Not only had it woken them up but also they were rightly concerned all this noise would wake their neighbours and make them very unpopular. The landlord telephoned the brewery, which at that time was Friary Meux just a few hundred yards away, demanding to know why on earth they were making a delivery in the middle of the night. The reply from the night staff on the other end of the line confirmed that not only had no delivery been ordered but also the brewery never made night-time deliveries for obvious reasons. The landlord then concluded that perhaps the pub had some very clumsy intruders. He went down the stairs through the pub and then down to the cellar. Just on the other side of the door the bangs and crashes were still continuing unabated. He reached out for the door handle, turned it, began to open the door – and suddenly there was silence.

The cellar was in darkness and not only was it deserted but not a single thing had been touched. Every barrel was in its place and nothing was amiss. Understandably, the landlord was stunned by his inexplicable finding but, knowing he was not going to find an explanation, he shut the door again and went back to bed. Unable to sleep because of the strange events of the night, he suddenly sat up as the bangs and crashes began all over again. He followed the same steps and was met with the same results upon finding an empty and orderly cellar when he opened the door. This happened yet once more during the night but this time he didn't go to check, as he knew what he'd find.

At the back of the Star is a function room for 100 people. This is where the punk band The Stranglers played their first ever concert in 1974, when they were still called The Guildford

The Star.

Stranglers. The Star is directly on the other side of the road to where the second and third Guildford Houses of Correction used to stand and it was in this room where Magistrates used to meet before crossing to the prison. The room is extraordinarily cold a great deal of the time, which must come as a welcome relief to the throngs of students who pile in there to hear local bands every week. Several people have also said there is a nasty atmosphere in the room. There are other vague stories about the bars in the pub being haunted by an unknown man but when I made enquiries, the staff were unable to give me any details.

Jonty's last night

The Yvonne Arnaud Theatre, Millbrook

Along the A281 road called Millbrook that leads to Shalford and on the banks of the River Wey, is the Yvonne Arnaud Theatre. It is named after the very popular actress and pianist Yvonne Arnaud, who lived at No. 35 London Road, died there on 20 September 1958 and is buried in the nearby yard of St Martha's Chapel. The theatre was opened in 1965 and is one of the most highly reputed provincial theatres in the country. What few people realise is that the theatre is built around the site of Guildford's sixteenth-century ducking stool, commonly reserved for the public humiliation of scolding wives, prostitutes and gossips.

The Yvonne Arnaud Theatre.

In the 1980s the front of house manager was a man called Jonty. Jonty was rather preoccupied, as a fortune-teller had told him – somewhat unprofessionally – that he would die before he reached his fortieth birthday. As Jonty was thirty-nine years and eleven months he was getting rather concerned. So much so, in fact, that he held his fortieth birthday party two weeks early as he was convinced he wouldn't be around to see the day itself.

The party came and went and all was fine. Jonty's fortieth birthday came and went and all was still fine. Two weeks later he suddenly keeled over and died. Shortly after his death the new front of house manager started hearing padding footsteps walking behind him backstage when he was locking up at night. It wasn't long before this was accompanied by the rattling of padlocks from doors he'd only just locked. Security guards still complain of hearing someone walking behind them, or feeling someone is close by, when on patrol at night. They've also stood in the auditorium in the early hours to hear feet walking across the stage. The staff think this is Jonty, locking up the building as he did on the last night of his life. The backstage crews have been known on occasion to dare each other to run through the backstage area in the dark after discussing Jonty's ghost.

A depressing place

The Mill Studio Theatre, Millbrook

Next door to the Yvonne Arnaud is the eighty-seat Mill Studio Theatre, opened in 1993. A mill has stood here since Medieval times but the current building was begun around 1770. Until

The Mill, c. 1905.

Millbrook was smashed through the area in 1961, a small winding lane that preceded it stopped here. During the early 1800s the mill had a very dark few years.

Between 1810 and 1811 it is claimed that no less than three millers committed suicide by hanging themselves from a beam on the first floor. The rope marks are reputed to still be there, next to the dates carved on the wall. In 1813 an apprentice was killed when the machinery caught his clothing and the following year the miller himself, Joseph Burt, was killed the same way. When chipping ice off the cogs in the middle of winter the machinery suddenly started up again and … well, you can imagine the rest.

Five violent deaths in the space of four years. It has been said that this has contributed to an odd feeling in the building. A feeling of not being alone, of being watched, of not being welcome. A feeling of overwhelming evil. And some people have had these feelings when they've not been watching an amateur show! It's also been said that dogs refuse to enter the building. Two employees were talking in the doorway in the 1990s when a dog with one of the men started growling, clearly distressed by something inside the building. This coincided with a sharp drop in temperature.

I know some people who were working in the Mill in 1996. They were in the dressing room on the first floor when they heard banging coming from the empty floor above them. This turned into stamping feet that marched over the entire length of the building, the footfalls being so heavy as it passed over them it caused dust to fall between the floorboards onto their heads.

A new pair of sandals, please

Millets, No. 21 Friary Street

The Dominican Order was founded in 1216 and five years later had set up its first house in England, near Oxford. Dominicans wore a black cloak and hood and it is from this that they gained their common name of Black Friars. Friars and monks are not the same thing. Monks would seek solitude from the world, whereas friars were poor and often learned men who would by nature have to be part of the community as a spiritual and practical service in order to survive.

The friary at Guildford was one of the smallest and poorest in the country, never housing more than twenty friars and only receiving a fortnight of food from the Royal coffers in its two hundred and fifty years. Far from being a superior lifestyle to those outside its walls, the friars lived primarily by begging from the locals. At the time of its dissolution by Henry VIII in 1538, only seven friars remained. The inventory shows nothing of value – a rare case of an establishment having actually remained true to its values and begging the question why such a place, clearly no drain on resources, was closed at all. What does not appear to be recorded is the box containing the heart of the seven-year-old heir apparent Prince Henry, in whose memory the friary had originally been founded in 1275. By 1600 most of the friary had been removed and what remained was largely in ruins. Like the Cistercian abbey at Waverley, much of the remaining stone was taken for building works at Loseley House and in 1630 the Earl of Annandale built a mansion there, which destroyed the floors of what was left and a great deal of the cemetery in creation of its garden. After this came barracks for the Militia. They moved out in 1818, eventually building a depot across the street. The old friary site served various uses throughout the nineteenth century. From 1890 Friary Meux occupied the site, which closed in the early 1970s. Construction of the shopping centre has entirely removed every single trace of the original buildings. Thankfully, the site was carefully recorded as far as possible before this happened.

Friary Street is indeed an ancient route that linked the friary to the lower part of the High Street and is recorded on maps from the 1600s. Although the main entrance to the Friary lay just beyond the outskirts of the town in Woodbridge Road, the public accessed the church for services from the south. At one time it was named Bear Lane because of the Bear pub which was a sixteenth-century timber building at No. 5. It was demolished at the end of the 1960s when Friary Street was pedestrianised but the front of the building still stands. One would think that The Friary Centre itself should have its fair share of cowled spectres but hardly any supernatural activity has been reported there.

The sightings of ghosts actually come from the south side of Friary Street. A monk in black with a hood pulled over his head has been seen walking through the wall at Woolworths and into Millets next door. It seems his face is never seen. An ex-employee of Millets informed me she believed the friar was responsible for knocking goods off the walls, breaking items in the shop and, on occasion, tearing off rucksacks that were tied into place. One Sunday evening as the shop shut she had been locking up the building and had seen a man in old-fashioned clothing walk past her out of the corner of her eye. The next day she was standing at the top of the stairs telling a colleague about what she'd seen the night before and as she looked down the stairs, the cowled friar was there just standing at the bottom, facing towards her.

Millets.

Interior designer

The Plough, Park Street

William Sparkes, a Guildford banker, built a row of cottages on land he bought along Park Street around 1810. A brewer, named Thomas White, bought them at the end of 1845 and so it is thought these cottages became the Plough public house from that time, staying in the White family for another half a century. It is a very small pub and sandwiched between some non-descript office buildings (replacing on one side some wonderful Tudor cottages pulled down in 1956) on the busy one-way system, it is very easy to miss.

On 11 February 2005 the landlord, Darren Walter, the barman, Dave Westlake and a few locals were discussing planned decoration work at the pub. A reproduction photograph of the pub 100 years ago was affixed to the wall to the right of the door and next to the bar. They watched astonished as it lifted itself from its nail, travelling 4ft forwards into the pub and then threw itself to the ground, smashing the glass. It was just the latest event in a series which had been plaguing Darren and his girlfriend Louise Flight, who had begun talking to the ghost in an attempt to persuade it to leave her alone.

They had taken over the pub in the early summer of 2004 and things had started soon after. Louise would often wake up in the night to find the jukebox in the bar had turned itself on

The Plough.

at the plug socket and was always playing the same song, though oddly she couldn't remember what it was. She claimed that one night she had to turn it off at the plug four times. One would think the simple answer would have been to remove the plug from the socket! The locals mentioned that they had understood a previous landlord had died from a heart attack and his ghost had occasionally been seen at the bar, drinking a gin and tonic.

Upstairs seemed to offer no respite from the hauntings either. Appliances in the landlord's flat had a habit of breaking down, the lights turned themselves off when Louise was in the bath and often people would close the sliding kitchen door only to watch it slide open again. All of these could possibly have natural explanations but the footsteps and door handles were another matter. Some people staying above the pub overnight have heard feet walking up and down the stairs and doors closing although everyone was in bed at the time and others have seen door handles moving up and down with no one on the other side.

I visited the Plough, upon request, with some of my equipment and interviewed Darren and Louise. They were both very pleasant and absolutely stuck to their stories without any embellishment or changes. However, I could find nothing in the way of strange electrical or magnetic fields in the building and didn't really feel it worthy of further investigation. I returned in January 2006 to take a photograph of the supposedly haunted picture frame. Not only had Darren and Louise left the previous month but also the pub had been redecorated and it was nowhere to be seen. The new landlord laughed, saying there was nothing in the pub and it was all 'a load of old rubbish'.

Chapter Three

OUTSIDE THE TOWN CENTRE

The Colonel

Avington, No. 31 London Road

In 2003 I was forwarded a letter from an old lady named Helen Bell. In the 1930s she had moved into a large house called Avington in London Road, just opposite Cross Lanes. It has now been converted into flats and two roads called Avington Close and Berkeley Court built around it. The family left the building at the end of the Second World War but the house still stands much as it was, surrounded by very sterile and new residential flats on three sides.

In 1937 Mrs Bell was at home by herself when an elderly man walked out of a room, straight past her and up the stairs. After recovering herself, she ran up the stairs after him only to find there was no sign of him. She told her husband, a doctor, when he returned home and his reply was suitably restrained. He said he was not surprised at all, as his own mother had frequently seen an old man walking along the landing on the first floor. The lady, certain of what she had seen and now bolstered by the story of other sightings, spoke to her neighbours about it. They too took it all in their stride. From the descriptions they told her they had no doubt that the old man was the original occupant of Avington, a Colonel Prendergast who had been very fond of the house.

Terror in the toilet

Automobile Association (demolished), London Road

Books are still being published referring to the AA building by the large roundabout on London and Boxgrove Roads. They don't seem to acknowledge the small issue that it was demolished over a decade ago! All that remains from that time is the old clock that now sits proudly on the current structure. The site is now occupied by a rather handsome building housing the company Baker Tilly and the staff there knew nothing about its previous history.

The Automobile Association built its office in Guildford, called Fanum House, in 1934. The company remained there for exactly fifty years, moving to Friary Street in the town in 1984 where it remained for about another ten years. Each book published on the ghosts in the old building seems to mention a different story but most refer to the haunted toilets on the first floor.

The lavatories were often heard to flush when they were empty and as word got around, some of the employees were wary of using the toilets. One night as a member of staff was turning off the lights around the building he thought he heard the voice of one of his female colleagues speaking in the toilet. He called out to her but there was no answer and he realised his colleague

Avington.

The AA Building. (David Rose Collection)

The offices of Baker Tilly.

was off duty anyway. Concerned that he may have encountered a trespasser, he alerted the security staff and they both pushed the door open to find it was deserted but the lavatory chain was swinging by itself.

A male member of staff who worked night shifts in the building would occasionally sleep in the building's rest room and noticed sometimes it would become inordinately cold and would adopt a strange atmosphere.

An apparition was infrequently seen – and heard – in the building. There were a few recorded sightings of a small and pale young woman who wore a grey or mauve (depending on which version you hear) skirt and was once heard to ask a member of staff, 'Can you help me?' She may also be responsible for the sound of footsteps that were heard. One night a security guard turned a corner and came face to face with her, before she faded away in front of him.

By the early 1970s the staff were all aware of the building's reputation and a few were secretly genuinely worried by it. Theories began that the ghost was that of a young woman who had drowned in a well that was once on the site. Certainly the water table was quite high and the building had a pump in the cellar at one time to keep it dry. One author has even suggested the young woman could be Lorna, who already has quite enough sites to her name!

One final account puts the hauntings down to a spectral cleaning lady in an old-fashioned apron who could also be heard emptying ashtrays, sweeping and dusting. Who would have thought dusting could be so noisy?

Take him away!

Various residential properties, Bushy Hill Estate

There is a story concerning a Council House in Guildford which was printed in many books on ghosts in the 1970s and became quite a local *cause célèbre*. The house in question could not really have been more innocuous or unlikely, for it stands in the middle of a sprawling housing estate in Bushy Hill, Merrow. The name of the street when first built was Finches Drive and the entire estate, close to the railway line to Clandon, was built around the area of Ganghill Common. This was a site of public executions in Guildford in the 1770s. Pamphlets still exist regarding two cases from that time.

Above: *Number 15 Finches Rise.*

Right: *Execution on Ganghill,*
August 1766.

A case that received a great deal of local coverage was the execution of three unrelated men (two of them highwaymen named James Potter and Frederick Gregg and the third a housebreaker called Christopher Ellis) on 26 August 1776. The men were taken from The House Of Correction at 11.00 a.m. and were praying at the execution site for half an hour before being hanged. The other surviving pamphlet concerns the life of Joshua Crompton, a forger, who was hanged at the same spot exactly two years later. It's been suggested that maybe No. 15 Finches Rise (a perfectly normal three-bedroomed semi-detached house from the 1950s) stands directly on top of the execution site, which may go some way to explaining the unsettling events of 1977.

The Fairweather family lived in the house and had suspected it of being haunted for two decades but until 1977 the strange goings on had only been a curiosity to them. For example, James Fairweather had previously seen a man wearing an old-fashioned costume with a long coat and black hat on one occasion and was known to dispel the ghosts by flicking towels in the air. Winifred Fairweather had once woken up and found the room was cold and she was pinned to the bed (though this almost certainly can be explained as sleep paralysis). Unusually, a flock of birds had taken to nesting in the attic. Visits by psychics, paranormal experts and priests had done nothing to lessen the events.

On 25 May 1977 the Fairweathers were woken by the sound of their grandson Jamie Hoare, who was two years old at the time, screaming during a thunderstorm. When his parents went to investigate he yelled at them, 'That's not my daddy! Take him away!' The hauntings had increased upon the birth of the Fairweathers' second grandson a few weeks before. The family, by all accounts, spent the night together in the living room and after one final bout of petitioning the Council to be moved were eventually granted new accommodation. It seems that nothing more happened at the house, so we can assume the hauntings were centred on the family rather than the building.

A fellow member of The Ghost Club, Sarah Darnell, worked for a nursing agency in Guildford in the 1990s. Her job generally involved community care work in order to maintain a degree of independence for the elderly and prevent them having to go into residential care. In October 1994 Sarah was looking after an old lady living in Bushy Hill Drive, the main road of the estate that actually encircles Finches Rise. Though now physically infirm the pensioner was nevertheless in full possession of her mental faculties.

During one visit – her last, as it turned out – Sarah found herself looking after the old woman late into the evening. The house had always had an uncomfortable atmosphere to it but this particular occasion was even more unwelcoming. Although the gas fire was on full and Sarah was standing very close to it, the bedroom had an unnatural coldness to it, as if a window had been opened. The old lady suddenly sat bolt upright in bed and fixed her gaze on an old green armchair in the corner of the room. In an act entirely out of character she suddenly snapped, 'Who's that man sitting in that chair?'

Sarah was momentarily too nervous to turn in case she were to come face to face with a spectre. The old lady pointed to the chair and said, 'Look! Can't you see him?' As Sarah finally managed to turn and confront whatever was there, the chair was deserted. She commented as much and as she did so the old woman suddenly returned to normal and had no idea she had just seen someone sitting in the chair. Whether or not she had actually seen a ghost we will never know. This is interesting because it gives us a brief insight into the psychology of paranormal experiences. It is perfectly possible the old lady was hallucinating but that does not mean that ghosts don't exist – it may just explain what a particular type of sighting actually is.

A few yards from Bushy Hill Drive, on the other side of the railway line, is Charlock Way. In the early 1970s another ancient spectre appeared in a modern house. A woman claimed that a golden haze had materialised in the hallway in her house and from it had appeared a man in Elizabethan costume. It is difficult to judge if this was a hallucination or another ghost. It seems unlikely that it would be the spirit of another hanged criminal, as in Elizabethan times executions were held elsewhere. There are also antiquated accounts of a spectral highwayman on a horse being seen in the area long before the site was developed.

Find me

Burpham Interchange, A3

Possibly the most unsettling of all Guildford ghost stories occurred very recently. One of the most chilling aspects of the case is the amount of people who had passed right by the fatal spot having no idea anything was amiss for nearly half a year and this will certainly have included myself. I have a vague recollection of passing the site at the actual time of the police recovery.

At 7.20 p.m. on 11 December 2002 several motorists called the Surrey Police after having seen either a car, or a pair of headlights, suddenly veering off the road and into the bank immediately after the sliproad leaving the A3 southbound at Burpham. The police went out to investigate and uncovered a mystery as bizarre as it is unnerving. Such a tale would usually make a great campfire ghost story but this was very real and happened within recent memory.

As they cleared away the scrub the police did indeed find a crashed car nose-down in a ditch. Though it was right next to the road, it was entirely masked from view by the vegetation. However, the contents of the recently wrecked Vauxhall Astra defied any explanation. In the driver's seat they found the victim, still strapped in. He was not injured but dead. The police could tell this quite quickly because the body was entirely decomposed and had been reduced to a skeleton. One officer described the discovery as 'spine-chilling'.

Enquiries through the car's registration and dental records of the driver eventually led the police to identify the remains as being those of Christopher Chandler, 21, from Isleworth. He was wanted in connection with a robbery and had been reported missing by his brother on 16 July that year. It had been assumed he had simply disappeared to avoid arrest. Vehicles had been speeding right past his body for half a year with no indication of what was just beyond the bank. Or had there been?

When the story broke of the ghostly re-enactment in the press, several people came forward saying they had seen stationary lights directly above the spot of the accident when passing at night. An alert from a dead man, or a manifestation of a will-o'-the-wisp? Either way, the police publicly confirmed they had been alerted to the spot by a reported sighting of an accident in December and that the car had been there for a considerable time.

Crazy horses

The Stables, Salt Box Road

It is not often that you hear ghost stories about local places you didn't even know existed but in 2003 I met a woman on my Ghost Tour by the name of Tina Cook. Along with four other

Salt Box Road stables.

people, she rents stables in Salt Box Road, north of the town centre. The structures have been there for many decades and it originally served as a pig farm. A friend of Tina's who died in April 2003 who also used the stables had told her that she had often seen 'orbs' there.

Most serious ghost hunters now largely – and correctly, in my opinion – dismiss orbs. During the boom in digital photography at the turn of the Millennium people started capturing strange white balls of light on their photographs which they had not seen with the naked eye. Many claimed these were photographs of ghosts and spirits and websites grew up all over the world dedicated to their study. The truth is far more mundane. These orbs are no more than dust, moisture and insects that are right next to the lens when the image is taken. It should be noticed that almost every orb photograph I have seen has been taken with a digital camera and all of them without exception have been taken with a flash. On a digital camera, the flash is so close to the lens that it causes these anomalies.

However, when orbs are seen for real – such as here – it is a different matter altogether. I myself have seen such things and we differentiate by referring to them as anomalous luminous patches, or ALPs.

Shortly before her death, Tina's friend and her brother went down to the stables very early in the morning to see if they could capture anything on film. There is no lighting or electricity on the site. The pair took hundreds of images in the hope of capturing something unusual and I have studied every one of them. On most, there is nothing irregular. There are plenty of orbs on the images that can be immediately dismissed as being very common photographic faults. However, several of the images presented me with something far more intriguing.

All the curious shots included very unusual and clear mist formations. The majority of them were far more spectacular than you would expect from just the illumination of breath vapour in the cold morning air. One of the shots had a 'vortex', or white pillar, filling up the left-hand edge. It had a straight edge to it, which one would not expect to find from human breath. Another image showed the eerie outline of a person beckoning towards the photographer's dog. The most spectacular image of all, however, has baffled photographic and paranormal experts alike. One very unsettling image shows the woman surrounded by a clear and symmetrical star of mist with what appears to be a face in the middle of it.

Tina's mother regularly goes down to the stables at 6.00 a.m. to feed the horses and sometimes none of them will go in the stables for their food, every one of them being disturbed by something. In January 2005 she was at the stables at dawn with her husband when he left her to do some work in a field 150 yards away. When she came out of the stables a man dressed in the style of a Cavalier walked straight past her. She spoke to him but he didn't reply. He walked around a corner and simply disappeared.

From one of the stables the sound of a woman humming has occasionally been heard. Not long after the Cavalier incident, Tina's mother had gone into that stable and set her torch down on a bale of hay while she loaded up a wheelbarrow for the horses. As she did so the torch was thrown several feet towards the door and broken. In August 2005 Tina and her mother were cleaning up in the stable yard when they clearly heard a woman calling them from the stables, although the stables were locked and they were alone. Several people have also heard footsteps walking down the main path of the stables only to find no one there. Tina's father once saw a woman in the stable compound and he called out to her to ask her what she wanted. She ignored him, set off around a corner and disappeared. Just beyond the stables is a bonfire site and sometimes people have been seen standing by it who have disappeared within a few moments.

Who's that girl?

Whitmoor Common, Salt Box Road

In the year AD 568 it is likely that Whitmoor Common was the site of the first recorded battle of Anglo-Saxon tribes in Britain. A gypsy stabbed another man there in November 1864 and in May 2005 it joined the long list of possible haunts of the infamous Surrey Puma, when two dogs chased a large cat-like animal up a tree.

I was contacted in 2005 by a retired police officer who had spent thirty years in the Surrey Police Force. Having no fear, he had often patrolled places like Brookwood Cemetery alone at night and had not once felt uneasy. In 1988, however, he had been walking his dog on Whitmoor Common – very close to the stables in Salt Box Road – at 10.00 a.m. when he saw a slim woman in a long dark grey coat walking towards him from about 100 yards away. He seemed to remember it was a tailored coat – not a cloak – with a wide hem and a hood but (as is so often the case) he does not recall seeing her face. His dog didn't seem to notice a thing. As the woman drew closer she suddenly diverted and walked behind a small clump of birch trees, over some scrub and past some tree trunks. She did not reappear on the other side and there was no other route she could have taken without being in full view. At the point when the man would have drawn level with her, the trees cleared again and the area was deserted. When he reached a cross in the paths he looked back to survey the whole open area and no one could be seen. He

Where the woman in black walks on Whitmoor Common.

mentioned to me as an aside that he had been involved in a murder case in the late 1980s in a garage off Worplesdon Road. The body had been found dumped on the common, though he didn't think there was any connection. He also vaguely remembered the case of a young woman from the WRAC who had been killed on one of the common paths in the 1960s.

This is not the sole sighting. There have been other reports of a ghostly woman walking by herself through secluded parts of Whitmoor Common, including one by a Mrs Thomas in the 1970s who saw her on exactly the same stretch of path upon which she was seen the following decade. Mrs Thomas lived on the adjoining road and was also startled some years ago by a man walking straight through her garden, oblivious to her. She reported he had been dressed in the style of a farm worker from a bygone age. A lot of Whitmoor Common has been cleared today and although I managed to find the exact spot, there is now no cover for about 100 yards or more in each direction. The clump of birch trees has been reduced to just three.

There are other gruesome stories concerning Whitmoor Common, which may well owe more than a passing debt to urban myth. One concerns the time when the common was used for army training exercises. Having insufficient overnight shelter, several soldiers decided to sleep underneath one of the trucks as it was pouring with rain. As it rained the ground turned to mud, causing the truck to sink and crush them all to death.

The two other tales relate to the train line that cuts through Whitmoor Common between Guildford and Worplesdon stations. It is banked very steeply on both sides and one account claims a navvy was crushed to death as the siding collapsed on this stretch of line. It has been said that he could be seen and heard trying to escape as his colleagues attempted in vain to reach him before he died. The other account says a railway employee fell from a train between Worplesdon and Guildford although his foot became caught on the train as he did so. Apparently his remains were found on the trackside for several hundred yards.

A gentleman who once worked on the common told me he had heard of people walking along the path bordering the railway line and hearing cries or moans coming from the bank. He also said when walking his dogs on that stretch of path they would refuse to walk anywhere near the fence.

The Navy lark

Pound Court sheltered housing (demolished), Wood Street

Pound Court was demolished late in 2005 to make way for eighteen affordable new homes for families and older people. In the same vicinity are a Listed farmhouse and a stream that occasionally floods. Opened in 1968, the scheme looked after old and vulnerable people but was deemed obsolete because of its outdated system of shared facilities in 2004. There were twenty-five one-bedroom flats on the site and when it closed some of them had been empty for up to a year with no waiting list. The manager, Anne Bailey, recalled one particular resident when it closed in the summer of 2005.

This old gentleman had been a chef in the Navy and used to amuse himself by playing small practical jokes on people. One thing he used to find funny was flicking fire extinguishers as he walked past them which would then create a small ringing sound. He would watch out of the corner of his eye and smile when people would turn their heads trying to figure out where the sound had come from. Shortly after his death the manager heard the ringing sound from the fire extinguishers again but there was now no one there to make it. It wasn't long after this that she was locking up for the night, closing curtains and turning off lights, when she glanced at the man's old chair and saw him sitting in it, smiling.

When I contacted Guildford Borough Council to ask them about Pound Court I was told that the buildings had been very ugly ones and though they searched their archives to try to find me a photograph they couldn't even find a brochure. They rightly pointed out that being a site with no aesthetic merit then there was little chance of finding any photos. The sad thing is, of course, that it is precisely for this reason that so many places are entirely lost forever.

Technically, a luvvie strop

Kadek House, No. 11 Woodbridge Meadows

Woodbridge Meadows is an area very close to the A25. It borders the railway line to London on one side and the River Wey on the other. There are rumours it was once used as a plague pit but this simply isn't true. There were two large houses in this area and Woodbridge Meadows was a large landscaped garden of one of them, destroyed in the 1880s when the rail tracks on a high bridge bisected it. It is now largely filled with industrial units. Kadek House was built as a printers in the 1960s. It is in three sections contained within two buildings and as the business went into decline the other units were let to external concerns. The final leaseholders moved out beginning in April 2005 and handed over the keys on 16 November. That leaseholder was the Guildford School of Acting, who used the site as its technical base where scenery was constructed. The building is currently empty and its future uncertain.

In June 2001 the master carpenter was closing up the lighting workshop for the day when she turned and saw a man in blue overalls standing in the corner who then disappeared. Her successor, Janet Williamson, saw the apparition herself in the same place exactly four years later.

In June 2003 Janet and one of her colleagues, Roger Ness, were working late at Kadek House preparing scenery for the GSA's production of *Annie*. On tidying the wood workshop they cleared away two large tables measuring 8ft by 4ft to the side of the room and placed covers on them when they swept the floor. The tables were very heavy and difficult to move and the brakes were on the castors. They left the building for the night and arrived back at work at 8.30 a.m. the following day. On entering the wood workshop half an hour later, they found that overnight the tables had been returned to their previous position.

Just over a year later a new wooden floor was ordered for the paintshop as previously it had only been partially boarded. The day before the new floor was scheduled to arrive, several of the staff spent some time lifting the dozen old planks and leaned them against a painting frame awaiting disposal. Though the building was locked and alarmed overnight, when they came back the next morning they found all the planks had been moved away from the wall and were all now stacked up neatly on the floor.

Shortly after this, Roger was working by himself in the paintshop on some scenery for a production of *Oliver!* when he heard a set of footsteps approaching him. They stopped and he looked up to see who it was but there was no one there. As he returned to work he heard six or seven more steps on the newly laid wooden floor.

In May 2005 the staff found a square of four ceiling tiles in a room upstairs near the back of the building had been pushed up out of their frame but a few days later they were back in place. Often people working in the building would hear a loud door slamming coming from the downstairs workshops which would be heard in the offices upstairs. It frequently happened and was usually heard in the early evenings. Sometimes two slams would be heard in rapid succession. Roger often felt uneasy in the building and when locking up alone would leave as quickly as possible.

It is interesting to note that Kadek House is very close to an electricity pylon and lies underneath high capacity power cables and close to electric railway lines and a river. Various scientific studies have been undertaken into the role such factors play in haunted buildings. I once took part in an investigation at a set of haunted Tudor almshouses on the Suffolk coast. The team noticed that the building was directly beneath where high power cables crossed telephone

Kadek House. (Roger Ness)

lines and there was a mobile phone mast nearby. These high electric fields can cause changes in perception. The question remains, however: does it cause hallucinations or does it facilitate the experience of genuine phenomena?

The Guildford Massacre

Guildown

Guildown is a fairly nondescript and quiet area lying just to the west of the A3100 Portsmouth Road. It was part of the area enclosed by Henry II in 1154 as part of Guildford Park, which was itself part of Windsor Great Park. You might think that any ghoulish tale concerning Guildown would post-date the enclosure by many centuries but it actually happened 118 years previously and marks a dark period in Guildford's history thought for many years to be no more than a legend. Even now, it cannot be confirmed the act ever actually took place. It is possible the story was simply a piece of common ecclesiastic propaganda – such records have blurred historical accuracy so often.

The relationship between the players in this story is confusing. Ethelred the Unready died in 1016. His widow Emma married the next King (Cnut) and her sons were exiled to France. When Cnut died in 1035 he nominated his son Harthacnut to be monarch but because Harthacnut was in Denmark his half-brother Harold took the reins.

Guildown from St Catherine's, c. 1905.

One of Emma's exiled sons, Alfred, came back from France to complain to his mother about the distortion of lineage priorities. He met with one of her advisors, Earl Godwin of Wessex and they rode to meet her at Winchester, stopping overnight at the royal lodge at Guildford. It is unknown where this might have been but the area around Holy Trinity church at the top of the High Street has been suggested. Certainly, it would not have been at Guildford Castle as that was built later.

During the night, the Earl of Wessex summoned his troops to seize the sleeping followers of Alfred. What happened next is unclear but the final result is undisputed. The prisoners were either bludgeoned where they slept, were twice decimated in the street, or were executed at Guildown. The *Anglo-Saxon Chronicle* makes the typically exaggerated claim that 600 men met their end this way, leaving only six survivors who were sold into slavery. Of Alfred, it is said, after being forced to witness the bloodshed he was blinded for his presumption in disputing the throne and died in captivity in Ely.

This was the gruesome story that by the twentieth century had been forgotten or, at best, dismissed. However, in late August 1929 John Kempster, who lived in Chalk Hill on Guildown Avenue, found two skeletons in his garden. Archaeologists found the deep burials of three dozen people with grave goods from the sixth century but far more chilling were the 186 bodies only 18 inches underfoot.

All had been cruelly dispatched. Some had been tied up and driven through with spears, others had been beheaded or dismembered, though we cannot dismiss the possibility that at least some of this was done by later ploughing. Nearly all of them showed signs of violent head trauma; many of the skulls had been caved in with swords or blunt instruments. The common consensus is that these are the earthly remains of the victims of the Guildford massacre. But … there is always a but: how could these men have been so easily taken *en masse* up to Guildown from the town to be killed? Why were the remains so far away? A partial answer is that a final act of cruelty could be achieved by burying the bodies in a Pagan site. It is also possible that locals might have taken the corpses away themselves, fearing the spirits of the slaughtered men.

To compound the inconsistencies, a coin was found with one of the skeletons which had been hammered ten years after the murders had taken place. This indicates that at least some of the people who met grisly ends in Guildford and were buried unceremoniously on Guildown did not die at the hands of Earl Godwin's men.

It is known executions were held close to this spot in antiquity and perhaps some of these haphazard burials, often interred in groups, might be connected to this and not the barbarity of 1036. It is likely there are many other bodies as yet undiscovered on the same site. As you would expect, the undisputed violent deaths that took place here so long ago have left their mark. Though people are thankfully spared a visual re-enactment, local legends say on still nights you can sometimes hear the agonised screams of men on Guildown.

The sound of chanting

St Catherine's Chapel, Portsmouth Road

St Catherine's Chapel is one of Guildford's better kept secrets. Most people will only see it if they stand on top of the motte of Guildford Castle and look south. The chapel can just be seen on a hill that rises on the right. It is a small sandstone structure of 50ft by 25ft, with a bell tower in one corner.

There are signs of human habitation there going back to the Mesolithic period – the oldest traces of life in the area – in the form of 3,000 pieces of worked flint. In medieval times St Catherine's Hill was called Drake's Hill, a derivation of Dragon's Hill due to the ancient legend a dragon lived under it. Curious how things go in circles, as anyone standing on the hill today may feel it shake under their feet. This is caused by the railway line to Portsmouth running right underneath it. The sand that makes up the hill caused the tunnel to collapse in spectacular fashion in March 1895. Twenty-two years previously, three people were killed in the shadow of the chapel when a train collided with a bull.

The chapel which tops the hill today was built in 1317 by Richard de Wauncey, the Rector of St. Nicholas church, in whose ownership the ruins remain. It was to be used as a 'chapel of ease' for parishioners who lived too far from Guildford to make the trip to church in Guildford each Sunday. However, as Artington is only about twenty minutes walk from the town and hardly anyone lived there anyway, the chapel saw very little use – possibly as little as once a year to keep its consecrated status.

Fairs were held on the hill during the Feast of St Matthew every year (originally September but changed to October in 1752) and these continued until the outbreak of the First World War. The chapel fell out of use in the fifteenth century, was used as a barn in the eighteenth century and was partially restored by the Austen family as a picturesque ruin in 1797. It was once even painted by Turner.

At the bottom of St Catherine's Hill, away from Portsmouth Road is the River Wey and next to the river is an ancient spring, which was mentioned as early as 1328 as, 'the spring of the glorious Katherine virgin and martyr'. The spring has for centuries been said to have miraculous curative properties, particularly for eyesight problems.

A grey lady has been seen emerging from the ruins (which are now surrounded by two sets of iron railings) and walking across St Catherine's Hill. On other occasions, the spectre has been little more than a mist. Several people in the 1970s and '80s took to sleeping up on the hill in the

St Catherine's Chapel in the early 1800s.

summer and all mentioned the exact same occurrence of the grey lady at different times. Grey ladies are very annoying as there are so many of them and are so often completely anonymous. There is often no known connection to the site.

Plenty of people on St Catherine's have heard the sound of chanting and a few have commented they have seen a nun walking across the hill. The fact that Langton Priory – still in use today – lies just at the bottom of St Catherine's Hill may go some way to explaining this, but you never know.

The good, the bad and the other one or two

Loseley House, Loseley Park

Loseley House was constructed from stone largely plundered from the dissolved Cistercian abbey at Waverley outside Farnham. It was built between 1562 and 1570 by Sir William More (distantly related to Chancellor Sir Thomas More) upon a personal demand from Elizabeth I. She had found the previous house on this site too small for her requirements and she was not a woman to be disobeyed. It includes paintings, tapestries and panelling taken from Henry VIII's spectacular lost palace of Nonsuch. Loseley also has a carved chalk fireplace of which Gaudí would have been proud. Some of the rooms are open to the public each summer, though the house remains as the family home of the More-Molyneuxs in whose line it has passed since inception. Queen Elizabeth, James I and Queen Anne have all stayed there. The west wing (containing a chapel, picture gallery and riding school) was demolished in the 1830s. In the latter half of the sixteenth century the Earl of Southampton was held prisoner here in the custody of Sir William. Old books refer to a blocked-up secret passage linking the dungeons here to ground level but, of course, there were no dungeons and the passage that emerged to the west is probably a drain.

Loseley's ghosts are mentioned in many books on the paranormal but details on them are rather scarce and that is the way the family prefer it. It is said that the reason details have never been particularly forthcoming is because the people who have seen things at Loseley are sworn to secrecy.

What all the books agree on is that there are three 'main' ghosts there. Firstly, they speak of an apparition known as the Pleasant Lady. A fine old portrait of this woman was discovered in the attic at Loseley but upon removal, she started to appear in spirit form. She was usually seen outside one of the bathrooms, smiling benignly. She was first seen by Mrs More-Molyneux in the 1970s and is said to be wearing smart brown clothing of the late Victorian era.

The Unpleasant Lady is, obviously, a less attractive encounter. The story dictates that she killed a child (of more anon) around 1600 and upon discovery of her crimes, her husband had her locked in a room for the rest of her life. It is claimed that on one date every year, agonised screams can be heard renting the air from that room. This is an example of a 'cyclic' ghost; a supernatural experience that happens on the same date each year. Other examples include the Ferryboat Inn in Holywell, Cambridgeshire, Bramber Castle in Sussex and Ham House in Richmond where a scream is heard from a window at the Site Manager's flat every 31 January (though not the two years I was there as an investigator). The woman has been seen at the bottom of a staircase and has been accompanied by a considerable drop in temperature. More frequently, however, she chooses to appear in one of the bedrooms and is said to be wearing a dark grey dress and has a scowl on her face.

The third ghost is the token confused account. It is either the Unpleasant Lady's stepson or her daughter. One version claims her young stepson stood in the way of an inheritance reaching her natural offspring and so she killed him by cutting off his leg (a most curious and obscure method of murder) so her own son could gain the fortune. The account more frequently referred to concerns the woman's daughter. She had the little girl drowned in the moat which once surrounded Loseley (and is still remembered in the name of Moat Cottages on the Loseley estate with a fraction of the southern side) but no accounts say why. Nor do any of them suggest any particular area of Loseley Park where the child is seen, or even why she is supposed to have a connection to the Unpleasant Lady.

There are other minor hauntings at Loseley. An American woman by the name of Dodge stayed at Loseley in 1913 and left after a single night because of something terrible she could not describe. A Victorian couple have been seen promenading around the grounds. A ghostly horse and carriage has been seen hurtling through the main gates. A man wearing fancy dress (or perhaps normal dress in his own period?) has been seen in the Long Gallery. Finally in the house, I have found one account of the daughters of the family some generations ago often seeing a kindly old lady sitting in a chair with a serene smile keeping watch on them in their playroom. As they grew up it dawned on them that something was amiss and they informed their parents. It seems the family were so scared upon realisation they had seen a ghost that they moved away and sold the house. As the Mores and the More-Molyneuxs have always owned Loseley we need to take at least part of this story with a hefty pinch of salt.

I was told by a local man that the More-Molyneuxs move out each winter and leave the house to the ghosts. He claimed that if you drove up to the house any night and looked at

Above: *Loseley House in the late 1800s.*

Left: *A very rare mid-Victorian photograph of the lake in Loseley Park.*

the windows you would see all the lights going on and off by themselves. This is, of course, a story entirely without any foundation.

In the grounds, we should also not forget that the ghost of Christopher Slaughterford was apparently seen there in 1709 after his execution in Guildford High Street. In 2001 I spoke to a woman whose son had been involved in an open-air show at Loseley a few years previously. Some distance behind the audience and seemingly uninterested in the spectacle, he had seen an old lady leading a donkey. She had walked up to a small clump of trees but didn't emerge from the other side. No one else had seen her and being on stage the gentleman returned to the task in hand. This story is particularly curious because the same manifestation has also been seen in Chinthurst Lane in Bramley, a couple of miles from Loseley. On old gypsy woman leading a donkey has been seen leading it along the side of the road. On one sighting in 1971 an airline pilot and his daughter saw them but the child could only see the donkey. As they reached the site of a medieval bridge over a stream (curiously at the bottom of the garden of author of the paranormal Andrew Green) they both disappeared. This may not be the same pairing of ghosts who were seen at Loseley but it is a remarkable coincidence.

In all, the sheer amount of spectres supposedly seen over the years at Loseley brings to mind the kind of 'true' ghost stories I read as a child which kindled my life-long interest in ghosts. In reading such books you only get to see buildings in one light and can be prone to forget that many years and decades can pass at any one of these sites with nothing strange occurring. The kind of haunted house you see in children's television programmes and dubious 'reality' shows is a very rare thing indeed. No building is always unsettling. On a bright sunny day even the most terrifying location — the type at which ladies appear at windows as a harbinger of death — is nothing more than a happy aesthetic excursion. We need to remember that the dark and spooky sides to buildings are just a small part of their existence.

Afterword

Ghosts do exist. I have seen at least one and had many supernatural experiences. What we need to address is what they actually are and – when the evidence can't be found – if there is any reason to believe some of the long-established stories about them. When authors abuse their position and write stories they know to be untrue, writers in the future pick up those stories and history becomes a distortion of the facts. I hope I have, at best, managed to be impartial and allowed you, good reader, to draw your own conclusions.

BIBLIOGRAPHY

Alexander, Matthew, *Guildford – A Short History*, Ammonite Books (Godalming) 1992

Alexander, Matthew, *Guildford As It Was*, Hendon Publishing (Nelson) 2000

Batchelor, Allen, *Guildford In 1908*, John J. Jones (Guildford) 1908

Chamberlain, E.R., *Guildford*, Phillimore (Chichester) 1982

Chapman Davies, Helen, *The Guildford Union Workhouse And The Vagrants' Casual Ward*, Guildford Borough Council (Guildford), 2004

Collyer, Graham & Rose, David, *Images Of Guildford*, Breedon Books (Derby) 1998

Forman, Joan, *The Haunted South*, Jarrold Publishing (Norwich) 1989

Green, Andrew, *Ghosts Of The South-East*, David & Charles (Newton Abbot) 1976

Green, Andrew, *Our Haunted Kingdom*, Fontana (Godalming) 1974

Green, Andrew, *Phantom Ladies*, Bailey Brothers & Swinfen Ltd (Folkestone) 1977

Green, Andrew, *Unknown Ghosts Of The South-East*, SB Publications (Seaford) 2005

Green, J.K., *Sidelights On Guildford History II*, J.K. Green (Guildford) 1953

Guildford Museum Excavation Unit, *Discovered A Mediaeval Synagogue in Guildford?*, Guildford Borough Council (Guildford) 1996

Innes, Brian, *The Catalogue Of Ghost Sightings*, Cassell (London) 1996

Janaway, John, *Haunted Places Of Surrey*, Countryside Books (Newbury) 2005

Jones, Richard, *Haunted Inns Of Britain & Ireland*, New Holland (London) 2004

Kelly's Directories Limited, *Kelly's Directory Of Guildford*, Kelly's Directories Limited (London) 1936–1975

Long, Roger, *Haunted Inns Of Surrey*, Conservatree Print & Design (Reading) 2002

Maxton, Caroline, *Foul Deeds & Suspicious Deaths In Guildford*, Wharncliffe Books (Barnsley) 2005

McMurray, Michael, *Ghostly Guildford*, The Surrey Magazine (Reigate) 2003

Newman, Stanley, *Guildford – The Changing Face*, Breedon Books (Derby) 2002

Nicholas, Roger, *…And The Lord Taketh Away*, Guildford Borough Council (Guildford) 2005

Poulton, Rob & Alexander, Mary, *Guildford's Dominican Friary: Recent Excavations*, Arrow Press (Aldershot) 1979

Rose, David, *Guildford Our Town*, Breedon Books (Derby) 2001

Russell, John, *The Guildford Jackdaw*, J. Russell (Guildford) 1794

Sandison, Pam & Lord, Frances, *All About And Round About St Catherine's*, St Catherine's Village Association (Guildford) 2001

Stewart, Frances D., *Surrey Ghosts Old & New*, AMCD Publishers Ltd (Purley) 1990

Sturley, Mark, *The Breweries And Public Houses Of Guildford*, Charles W. Traylen (Guildford) 1990

Unknown, *The Guilford Ghost*, A. Hinde (London) 1709

Unknown, *Tryals of The Most Notorious Malefactors For Near 50 Years Past*, T. Pathe (London) 1721

Other local titles published by The History Press

Haunted Suffolk

PETE JENNINGS

From heart-stopping accounts of apparitions, manifestations and related supernatural phenomena to first-hand encounters with ghouls and spirits, this collection of stories contains spooky tales from around the county of Suffolk. Over 150 locations – including the Eagle Street poltergeist in Ipswich and the abbey ruins' Brown Monk and Grey Nun in Bury St Edmunds – feature here to create a spine-tingling collection of supernatural tales.

0 7524 3844 1

Haunted Hastings

TINA LAKIN

This collection of stories contains new and well-known spooky tales from in and around the town of Hastings. From the haunted staircase at Hastings library in Claremont and the singing spectre of Hastings College, to the mysterious witches' footsteps in the Stag Inn and the phantom coach and horses that gallops up the High Street on a dark winter's night, this phenomenal gathering of ghostly goings-on is bound to captivate anyone interested in the supernatural history of the area.

0 7524 3827 1

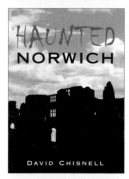

Haunted Norwich

DAVID CHISNELL

Contained in this selection are stories of the old witch who wanders up and down Bishopsgate, the lonely monk who can still be found strolling beside the graveyard at St John Maddermarket, and others who are said to haunt the city's infamous Tombland area. This fascinating collection of strange sightings in the city's historic streets and buildings is sure to appeal to anyone who would like to know more about the haunted heritage of Norwich.

0 7524 3700 3

Haunted Lincolnshire

DANIEL CODD

Drawing on historical and contemporary sources *Haunted Lincolnshire* contains a chilling range of ghostly tales. From accounts of spectral monks at Lincoln's medieval Cathedral and the highwayman who wanders the old coach yard of the fourteenth-century White Hart Hotel, to stories of the Green Lady at Thorpe Hall and sightings of the demon dog known as Black Shuck, this phenomenal gathering of ghostly goings-on is sure to appeal to those interested in the supernatural history of the area.

0 7524 3817 4

If you are interested in purchasing other books published by The History Press, or in case you have difficulty finding any of our books in your local bookshop, you can also place orders directly through our website
www.thehistorypress.co.uk